ALL YOU NEED TO KNOW ABOUT THE BIBLE

Book 5:
sense as well as faith

BRIAN H EDWARDS

DayOne

© Day One Publications 2017

ISBN 978-1-84625-588-5

All Scripture quotations, unless stated otherwise, are from The Holy Bible, New International Version Copyright © 1973, 1978, 1984 International Bible Society

British Library Cataloguing in Publication Data available

Published by Day One Publications
Ryelands Road, Leominster, HR6 8NZ
Telephone 01568 613 740   Fax 01568 611 473
North America Toll Free 888 329 6630
email—sales@dayone.co.uk
web site—www.dayone.co.uk

Cover design by Kathryn Chedgzoy
Printed by T J International

ALL YOU NEED TO KNOW ABOUT THE BIBLE

BRIAN H EDWARDS

Book 5
Sense as well as faith

The series outline

Book 1 Can we trust it?
What this book is all about

1. **What's the Bible all about?**
   The Master Plan with Jesus Christ as the theme
2. **Remarkable prophecy**
   What do we do with these incredible predictions?
3. **Evidence of an eyewitness**
   Proof that the writers were there
4. **Did Jesus really live?**
   Jesus fixed in history
5. **Living letters for living churches**
   Marks of real letters to real Christians
6. **Fact or fiction?**
   Evidence of the Old Testament written in its time

Book 2 Big claims from a unique book

1. **The God who reveals himself**
   Evidence everywhere
2. **Ultimate truth**
   God-given and without error
3. **Jesus and his Bible**
   What Scriptures did Jesus use?
4. **The apostles and their Bible**
   What Scriptures did the apostles use?
5. **Absolute authority**
   Big claims by prophets, Jesus, and apostles
6. **Is the Bible enough?**
   Sufficient and final
7. **The Chicago statement**
   The inerrancy statement of the International Council for Biblical Inerrancy

Book 3 Have we got the right books?

Book 4 A journey from then to now

Book 5 Sense as well as faith

1. Tearing the Bible apart
The Bible and its critics

2. Great minds on a great book
What scholars say

3. Digging up the evidence
Archaeology confirms the truth

4. Guidelines for combat
Errors and contradictions?

5. Solving the problems
Resolving some of the issues

Book 6 Enjoy your Bible!

1. It's for you, it's alive—read it!
The best way to read the Bible

2. Reading the Bible with common sense
A guide to a good understanding

3. A bit more common sense
Types, symbols and dangers to avoid

4. Getting to grips with the Old Testament
A chart of the books in their proper place

5. Piecing the Gospels together
A harmony of the life of Jesus

6. Where did they write their letters?
The Acts of the Apostles and where all the letters fit in

7. Reading the Bible from cover to cover
A careful plan to read it all in eighteen months!

8. Take time with God
Spending time each day with God

Contents

Series outline

What this book is all about

The Bible is not a book of low moral standards that encourages people to rebel against governments and rulers. It's not the Bible that spawns terrorism, supports corruption or cheers the idle. On the contrary, no book has ever been written that maintains such a consistently high standard of morality. For the past two thousand years, untold millions of Christians have taken this book as their rule and guide for life. They have gladly obeyed it and readily died for it.

Why then has the Bible been so bitterly attacked? One answer is that it makes great claims for itself. It claims to be the word of the only true God and therefore to carry the authority of the Creator with its every sentence and line. It also claims to be the only totally reliable guide to tell us all that we need to know about God, the origin of the universe, the beginning of the human race, the meaning of life, what happens beyond the grave, and the way to find friendship with our Creator. The Bible demands that its laws and statements must carry more authority than those of any government, church or religion. It also claims that its history, geography, and any other subject it deals with, are accurate and more valuable than any of the theories of men. The Bible never claims to be just one book among many, but the book above all. 'As for God, his way is perfect; the word of the Lord is flawless' (Psalm 18:30). Claims like this are not popular.

Book five begins by tracing the history of Biblical criticism. What were the influences, in every academic discipline, that led to a destructive view of the Bible? And what have been the strengths and weaknesses of evangelical Christians in responding?

Those who read the Bible are often intimidated by what one critic called, 'the tyranny of untested assumptions', and the impression is given that only academics can properly understand the issues that lie behind criticisms against the Bible. This book exposes some of those untested assumptions and reduces complex issues to an accessible level.

It is encouraging to move from this negative information to the positive of what some of the most brilliant academics in the world of biblical archaeology have concluded. A commitment to biblical authority is a commitment to sense as well as faith. In chapter 2 the focus is on some for whom the force of truth radically changed their earlier opinions, but at centre stage are two great scholars whose work still speaks powerfully of their challenge to those who question the historical accuracy of the Bible. Their conclusions have been confirmed, but not surpassed, by modern archaeologists, and no Christian needs to be ashamed to quote from two outstanding scholars of last century. One concluded, 'I try to give my students such an intelligent faith in the Old Testament Scriptures, that they will never doubt them as long as they live. I try to give them *evidence* … I have now come to the conviction that no man knows enough to assail the truthfulness of the Old Testament.' The other affirmed, 'Christianity did not originate in a lie, and we can and ought to demonstrate this, as well as to believe it.'

Some of the clear archaeological evidence supporting the accuracy of historical statements is offered in chapter 3. This may be familiar ground for some, but here the subject has been brought up to date. Few of those who dismiss the Bible are aware of the vast amount of evidence, accepted by archaeologists of every persuasion, that supports even some of the most detailed statements in the Bible. One undisputed master of the study of cuneiform texts concluded, 'Archaeology, correctly understood, always confirms the accuracy of the Bible.'

However, there are serious questions to be answered. The challenge of those apparent errors and contradictions that are found occasionally—and only occasionally—in the Scriptures, must be answered. Under the heading 'guidelines for combat', a chapter presents some of the principles that are helpful in understanding how to respond. Christians need not be afraid to face up to such questions as: 'Do we need to defend inerrancy anyway?', 'Is harmonising justified?', 'Do we have the actual words of Jesus?' and even, 'Are there lies in the Bible?' The chapter also considers alternative ways of responding to the critics—some wise, some unwise.

Finally, examples of possible errors and contradictions are considered. In presenting possible solutions, some important principles are discovered that will equip the Christian for answering the critic. It is not necessary to *prove* an answer to every criticism, it is sufficient for a *reasonable* answer to be given. Not one of the narratives in the Bible tells us everything that took place, and the records of conversations and instruction, whether by Jesus or anyone else, are certainly not necessarily transcriptions of everything that was said.

As the series draws to a close in the final book it is vital that we never look at the Bible simply as a book to be attacked or defended. Remember, the Bible is not a battlefield but the pathway into life. For this reason, the last book in the series is entitled *Enjoy your Bible!* The best way to read our Bible, how to understand it with sound common sense, and how we can read it in its historical context will encourage us to spend more time with God and his word each day.

1. Tearing the Bible apart

The Bible is the most 'persecuted' book ever written, but the fact that it has withstood the attacks, and for two thousand years has remained the handbook of the Christian faith for countless millions of readers, is testimony to its truth and value.

G overnments destroy it, philosophers dismiss it, scientists ridicule it, the media parody it and today most in our western society ignore it. But the Bible is still the world's best-selling book and nothing can equal its power to change lives.

In the introduction to this series the question was asked, why has the Bible, though so popular, been so attacked by its critics? Part of the answer was that it is the result of the claims of the Bible itself, not least its claim to be the word of God and without error. That is sufficient to goad many into a denial. To accept it, demands obedience.

For two centuries following the Reformation, the Bible was generally accepted and respected in Britain, much of Europe and across North America. Those who criticized or denied its authority were a small minority. The Enlightenment in the mid-seventeenth century, following the restoration of the monarchy, impacted trust in the Bible. Frances Schaeffer described the Enlightenment as 'In general, an intellectual movement which emphasised the sufficiency of human reason and scepticism concerning the validity of the traditional authority of the past.'[1] In the church of the eighteenth century it led to widespread deism—a distant and unconcerned God who had little or no interest in personal religion. This was slowed, but not halted, by the spiritual revival (the 'Great Awakening') under Wesley, Whitefield and many others. During the latter half of that century and throughout the nineteenth, a number of influences began to change

---

1 Francis Schaeffer, *The Great Evangelical Disaster* (Crossway. Wheaton Il. 1984), p. 33.

the attitude of many towards the Bible; today it is popular to ridicule the Bible and 'scholarly' to discredit it.

Nineteenth century influences against the Bible

PHILOSOPHY AND POLITICS

Two German philosophers, Immanuel Kant (1724–1804) and Albrecht Ritschl (1822–1889), doubted the supernatural and all statements of authority and certainty; they insisted that experience is the only proper basis to judge anything. Kant and Ritschl were sceptics—doubting everything. A third German philosopher-theologian, Friedrich Schleiermacher, published a book in 1821 with the innocent-sounding title: *The Christian Faith*. In it he stressed the importance of subjective feelings, over against authoritative statements, as the way of arriving at a knowledge of the truth. Doctrines, and supposedly infallible statements, had no place in these philosophies. Similarly, Søren Kierkegaard, a Danish philosopher born in 1813, taught that an individual's experience (existentialism) was what carries authority and meaning, and not external standards of belief or practice.

These philosophies had a great influence on the way people began to view all authority. The Bible was under attack. Men felt they were growing up in wisdom and they wanted to free themselves from anything limiting that freedom. This attempt to be free from rules and authority marched in company with a strong confidence in the ability of man to reason things for himself. Although the Scottish philosopher David Hume had died in the previous century (1776), his 'rationalism', which exalted human reason above everything, dispensed with the supernatural and therefore the miraculous. A large part of the Bible could now be discarded.

Although he could hardly be expected to understand the complex minds of German philosophers, the working man in Britain was stirring into action. Progress towards socialism with such movements as The Society for Promoting Working Men's Associations and The Christian Social Union, were a threat to the status quo. The recent whiff of gunpowder and the chopping of the guillotine across the Channel hardly reassured the minds of the authorities early in the nineteenth century, and by the middle of that century the fear of 'Red Republicanism' was real.

For his part, the working man considered that the 'Church' (meaning the Church of England) had failed him—which it had—and therefore the Bible had little to say to him. If the Bible had given birth to the Church, it was as irrelevant as its child. Inevitably by 1844 the British Anti-State-Church Association was formed with the avowed aim of separating church and state, and by 1912 The Labour Church Movement, which began as a 'Christian' political movement, had dropped all reference to God.

Never had there been such a torrent of new thinking pouring into the mind of the nation—and what a man thinks, he becomes. Slowly at first, and then more rapidly, the authority of the Bible was nudged out of the way. An army of ideas invaded the nineteenth century: Rationalism (David Hume 1711–1776), Existentialism (Søren Kierkegaard 1813–1855), Pragmatism (William James 1842–1910), Agnosticism (Herbert Spencer 1820–1823), Nihilism (Friedrich Nietzsche 1844–1900), and Communism (Karl Marx 1818–1823) were at the forefront of shaping the nation's mind. And each of them had an impact on the authority of the Bible.

SCIENCE AND DISCOVERY

At the same time, new frontiers in science and geography were opening. In 1780 the first cotton mill was built in the north of England, and England led the world into the 'Industrial Revolution'. It was confidently expected that this would bring mankind into the golden age of prosperity. The nineteenth century was also the age of discovery. Steam power, railways, electricity and the telegraph made men proud of their achievements. Someone could now travel round the world five times in a year. Everything, including God and his laws, could be judged by man's intellect and reason. Atheistic humanism grew stronger, replacing God by man, who was quite capable of working out his own future.

It was also the age of colonialism. In 1800 one third of the globe was barely known to the Western nations; a century later the whole world was open, and European countries were scrambling to extend their territory.

In Britain, it was the dawn of the golden era of Queen Victoria's empire on which the sun never set.

After the Battle of Waterloo in 1815, Englishmen were confident that the 'thin red line' of British regiments were invincible in the field. Not even the miserable Crimean war and the ghastly Indian Mutiny in the middle of the century, nor the terrible losses in the Zulu campaigns later, and the reverses in the Boer War at the turn of the century, could do more than dent this confidence in British supremacy. Britannia ruled the waves—and a quarter of the world's land as well. The undergirding philosophy was that man—especially the Englishman—could do anything and he did not need God to guide him. The Bible was the greatest enemy to this kind of thinking and therefore it had to be attacked.

ARCHAEOLOGY AND LITERATURE

The nineteenth century was also an age of renewed interest in the past. The very freedom that the Reformation had brought with it encouraged men to challenge, enquire and think independently. As a result, men wanted to know about the origins of everything; therefore 'Libraries were ransacked for hidden documents and the earth itself for the remnants of lost civilizations.' During the middle of the century British, French and German archaeologists were working in Egypt. In 1865 the Palestine Exploration Fund was set up, and in 1880 the Egyptian Exploration Society commenced. The Middle East and Asia were being plundered for pottery, inscriptions and all the rubbish left behind by long-lost civilizations. Archaeology was coming into its own as a science. Now, at last, we could find out the truth, or otherwise, behind the Bible stories.

Many history books were written, such as *The History of Civilization in England*, published in 1858 by the historian Henry Buckle, and in 1876 George Smith published Assyrian and Babylonian accounts of creation and a flood; this threw light, and for some doubt, on the biblical records; later his *Historical Geography of the Holy Land* opened up the Bible lands for the first time to the ordinary reader. Ancient moral laws, like the Hammurabi Codes, were discovered that were thought to predate Moses and from which Moses obtained his ideas for a law book for the Israelites.

Alongside all this, new ideas of literary criticism were coming to the fore which allowed the Bible no privileged exemption from the rigorous scrutiny of scholars eager to make their mark by sitting in judgement on the Bible just as on any other piece of literature.

GEOLOGY

In 1830 a Scottish lawyer turned geologist, Charles Lyell, published *Principles of Geology*, in which he claimed to have found evidence that the earth was much older than the Bible seemed to imply. In 1844 another book, this time by Robert Chambers but published anonymously and titled *Vestiges of the Natural History of Creation*, denied biblical creation and suggested a gradual development of the earth and universe under divine guidance. It was hugely popular, became a best-seller, and prepared the public mind in 1859 for Charles Darwin's *On the Origin of Species by Means of Natural Selection, or the Preservation of Favoured Races in the Struggle for Life*.

Borrowing from these previous works, Darwin popularised the idea that new species developed by cross-fertilization and mutations and that this was a natural, but very slow process within nature, taking place over millions of years. Certain qualities, Darwin taught, are favourable to survival, like strength, speed and colour; animals lacking these will die. By various changes (mutations), new abilities are developed, such as wings, legs or lungs.

This process of 'natural selection' was the foundation of Darwin's theory of evolution. It became a popular theory, was presented as fact, and soon included the whole of human existence. In Darwin's *The Descent of Man* in 1871, morality and religion were said to have 'evolved' from that which was simple and primitive to that which is detailed and complex. The Bible was seen merely as a book reflecting man's growth from a primitive religion to one far more complex; revelation was not needed. In 1869 T H Huxley popularized Darwin's evolutionary views and coined the word 'agnostic' (from Greek meaning 'without knowledge') to refer to those who believe that even if there is a God, the evidence for, and knowledge of, such a being is unknowable.

The effect of all this was to persuade first the universities and through them the preachers and then the men and women in the pew and on the street, that the Bible was simply another ancient history book which was interesting but could be right or wrong—mostly wrong. The philosophers insisted we must test everything by reason and avoid all authoritative statements. The historians and archaeologists claimed to have discovered sufficient information about ancient civilizations, and the way in which stories were passed down from one generation to another, to be able to question the accuracy of the Bible. At the same time, the scientists were certain that they knew how the world began, which was not at all like the biblical account. By the end of the nineteenth century there were apparently enough experts to confirm how little of the Bible we could trust. At this point another, and most devastating, influence on the church came into play.

THEOLOGY

At the University of Tübingen in Germany, a group of theologians had already begun to read the Gospels and Acts, not as historical accounts of what actually happened, but what they called 'the product of communal imagination', which roughly meant, 'how the early Christians would have liked it to have happened'. Two university professors, Ferdinand Christian Baur (1792–1860) and David Friedrich Strauss (1808–1874), introduced the word 'myth' to refer to the gospel stories. Strauss later renounced Christianity altogether. They admitted that Christ was historically real, but suggested that all the stories were made up to illustrate the way the early Christians thought about him. The task of the scholar was to strip away this myth to find the real truth at the centre. This was called 'demythologizing', a term later used by the Bible critic Rudolf Bultmann; it was like peeling off the outer layers of an onion, to discover the truth at the heart of the story.

The word 'myth', for theologians then and now, does not mean lies or fairy tales, but serious stories made up to illustrate spiritual truths. Those who say that the Bible contains myth are not suggesting that the early writers set out to deceive us, since, in the view of these theologians, they did not necessarily intend their history to be taken as literally true; they were merely presenting spiritual truths in a picture form. Apparently, they thought we would all know this. Of course, only the scholars were capable of stripping off these myths for us to find the real history, and ordinary Christians were expected to wait until the professors of Tübingen in Germany or Oxford in England told them what they could believe. To a greater or lesser extent this was the critical approach to the New Testament: the supernatural and miracles were abandoned and most of the New Testament writers were robbed of the books they claimed to have written.

Julius Wellhausen (1844–1918) was the Old Testament counterpart of Baur and Strauss. In 1878 he published his *History of Israel*, which is still a basic textbook for what is known as 'higher criticism'. Wellhausen believed that the first five books of the Bible, known as the Pentateuch, were written by several different authors, and at a late date were put together by various editors.[2] David was robbed of most of the psalms, at least two different men wrote Isaiah, and all Old Testament prophecy was assumed to have been written as late as possible—this avoided the embarrassment of having to take seriously prophecies that were fulfilled. In England, the Old Testament scholar Samuel Davidson (1806–1898), and others, followed the same route as Wellhausen. As with the New Testament, these academics assured the public that the Bible, though interesting and valuable, was like all other ancient books, and therefore was liable to contradictions and errors.

This is a small sample of what was happening at this time. It was now the task of the scholars to discover where the Bible could be trusted and where it could not.

---

2 Briefly, this is known as the 'documentary hypothesis' or JEPD theory. Sections of the Pentateuch that contain the divine name Yahweh, those that use Elohim (God), others containing the Priestly sacrifices and those that added the Deuteronomic code (Law), were each written and edited by a different hand. There has never been any full agreement among the proponents as to which parts of the Pentateuch belong to which editor. The 'documentary hypothesis' has largely fallen out of favour today although the hypothesis is still quoted as fact by some.

The Evangelical response

Since these influences, the storm has not slackened. In fact, the opponents of a trustworthy Bible have become more bold and vigorous in their sustained onslaught against the reliability of Scripture. A succession of responses by evangelical Christians will bring us to the present day.

HESITATION IN THE LATE NINETEENTH CENTURY

By the 1880s it was claimed, 'No periodical is complete without an article in which Christianity is defended or attacked.' Davidson, for example, in 1857 was forced to resign his post at the Lancashire Independent College in Manchester because of his liberal views. On the other hand, many Christians failed to study carefully the claims of the critics and they simply accepted the conclusions. Others tried to begin with the principles of what were known as the Higher Critics and argue back to an evangelical position. This proved impossible. With some notable exceptions, evangelicals were timid and lacked the intellectual vigour to combat the academics in Tübingen and Oxford.

Preaching lost its importance in the churches and consequently spiritual life and church attendance began slowly to decline. The High Church movement invested in impressive church architecture in a vain attempt to win back the disillusioned, and tragically many evangelicals lost their belief in the Bible as a book without error—or they retreated into a stubborn resistance without knowing how to answer the critics.

Very few realized what was happening until it was too late. Among those who did see the danger was Charles Haddon Spurgeon, England's most popular preacher of the Victorian era, whose regular Sunday evening congregation in London numbered around six thousand and whose printed sermons averaged around 30,000 each week. Spurgeon refused to accept either the principles upon which the critics worked or the conclusions to which they came, and he urgently warned evangelicals to hold fast to their belief in a Bible that can be trusted. His first warning came in 1887: 'Read those newspapers which represent the Broad School of Dissent, and ask yourself, How much further will they go? … The atonement is scouted, the inspiration of Scripture derided, the punishment of sin is turned into fiction, and the resurrection into a myth.'[3]

Seeing the downgrading of Scripture within the Baptist denomination, Spurgeon resigned from the Baptist Union in 1887. At the time he was cruelly vilified, but history proved the truth of his accusations; the Baptist Union, along with all the Free Church denominations, slipped steadily into the Higher Critical mould. Spurgeon was certain that time would prove many of the principles and conclusions of the critics to be wrong. In this also, Spurgeon was correct, but few leaders listened to him. However, even the normally incisive Spurgeon did not grasp the full danger of the evolutionary theories of Darwin.

CAPITULATION IN THE EARLY TWENTIETH CENTURY

At first evangelicals had few scholars to defend the reliability of the Bible and those who did were largely ignored. By 1909 a series of articles was being published in North America under the title *The Fundamentals*. These defended the long-held conservative evangelical view of Scripture and the term 'fundamentalist' was coined. In America, able scholars like Benjamin Warfield[4] and Gresham Machen were defending biblical authority, and in 1929 some of them left Princeton University to found Westminster Theological Seminary as a protest against the American downgrade.

In England, the influence of a new philosophy hastened the slide into a lack of confidence in the Bible. Logical Positivism, taught by men like Ludwig Wittgenstein (1889–1951), Moritz Schlick (1882–1936), and A J Ayer (1910–1989) in his book *Language, Truth and Logic* (1936), asserted that unless a statement can be proved either true or false, it is meaningless. Since many of the great claims of the Bible concerning God and salvation are not capable of being 'proved' in scientific terms, much of the Christian faith was considered to be irrelevant.

Gradually, all the major denominations slipped into the fashion of denying full authority to the Bible. Aided by two world wars, church

---

3 *The Sword and Trowel*, the magazine of the Metropolitan Tabernacle where Spurgeon was minister, August 1887.

4 See in this series Book 2 chapter 2 for Warfield's understand of Scripture.

attendance slid even further, and there was very little literature from an evangelical standpoint to stem the tide of unbelief. One man, among others, who was aware of this twentieth-century downgrade in Britain was E J Poole-Connor (1872–1962). As a pastor, mission leader, theologian and founder in 1922 of what is known today as the Fellowship of Independent Evangelical Churches, he had a firm grasp of what was happening in the evangelical world. In 1933 he published a little book under the title *The Apostasy of English Non-Conformity* in which he exposed the denominational leaders who had capitulated to critical views of the Bible.

In 1925 Dr Reaveley Glover, the incoming president of the Baptist Union, had reflected on Spurgeon at the time of his leaving the Union and concluded, 'Gout, conscience and Satan make queer alliances in us all.' Glover rejoiced in 'modernism'—the name for the critical attitude to the Bible—as a glorious 'holding open of the door for new conceptions of truth', and claimed that the idea that the whole Bible was inspired by God was a 'monstrous belief'.[5] Glover also denied the atonement of Christ and justification by faith as understood by the Reformers.

Arthur Samuel Peake, an Oxford don, president of the Free Church Council in 1929 and Principal of the Primitive Methodist training college, published *Peake's Commentary on the Bible* which was a thorough endorsement of modernism.[6] By the 1930s the conservative evangelical faith was not represented in any of the seven Methodist colleges in Britain.[7] Dr Fairbairn, a leading Congregational scholar, followed the same road, and the publication by the Baptist College Principal, Dr Wheeler Robinson, *The Religious Ideas of the Old Testament*, in which he adopted the liberal view of biblical history, was recommended reading for all students.

The issues in every case were not only academic debates about the accuracy of biblical history, but the inerrancy of Scripture, the reality of the virgin birth, the miracles of Jesus and his literal bodily resurrection,

---

5 E J Poole-Connor, *The Apostasy of English Nonconformity* (Thynne & Co Ltd, London 1933), pp. 26–30, 45–56.
6 As above, pp. 34–44. It should be noted that as a result of the liberal teaching of Arthur Peake, the Primitive Methodists lost their theological way and in 1932 re-united with Methodism.
7 As above, p. 58.

the substitutionary atonement and much more. Yet evangelicals still often failed to appreciate what was happening; even Dr Fullerton, a conservative evangelical, spoke of Reaveley Glover as a 'prophet whom God has sent us.'[8]

By the end of the first quarter of the twentieth century, not one free church denominational theological college in England was free from critical views of the Bible. Dr Reaveley Glover had chided conservative evangelicalism as being 'obscurantist'. Poole-Connor responded in 1933 by suggesting, 'Today, if you want a real old obscurantist college, you have to found a new one.' In 1946 the London Bible College was established.

Until the formation of the Bible Churchmen's Missionary College in Bristol (founded 1925, later best known as Tyndale Hall) and Oak Hill College, north of London (founded 1932), which became bastions of conservative evangelicalism, the situation was hardly better among the Anglican training colleges. By the 1920s the older evangelical Anglican colleges had mostly adopted a brand of Liberal Evangelicalism.

It is against this background that the strong stand made by many conservative evangelicals against the continuing downgrade in all the denominations leading to the watershed divide in 1966 must be understood.[9]

ASPIRATION TO THE MID-TWENTIETH CENTURY

From the end of the Second World War there was a new evangelical intellectual vigour. Through the influence of men like Martyn Lloyd-Jones, preaching at Westminster Chapel in London, and John Stott with his wide and popular preaching and writing ministry, some evangelicals took heart and fought back. The Inter-Varsity Fellowship (later the Universities and Colleges Christian Fellowship), and its associated publishing company InterVarsity Press, captured the minds of many Christian students; the Banner of Truth Trust reprinted long-forgotten Puritan books; the London Bible College set out to train ministers and missionaries; and the study centres at Tyndale House and Rutherford

---

8   As above, p. 45.
9   For more on this see Iain H Murray, *Evangelicalism Divided—a Record of Crucial Change in the years 1950–2000* (Banner of Truth, Edinburgh 2000).

House provided opportunities for evangelical research. All this appeared to promise a new and bright future for evangelicalism. Each stood firmly for a Bible without error.

Evangelicals were determined to take the ground away from critical scholars and redeem it for a high view of the authority of the Bible. Gradually, from the 1950s, evangelicals found places within the theological and biblical departments of national universities; they were to be found in all the disciplines, including archaeology. These were men of high intellectual ability (men like F F Bruce and D J Wiseman) and the motive was good: to meet modernism on its own ground—and to win.

Across the Atlantic, a similar attempt was being made to meet the challenge of the critics as evangelicals emerged from their 'fortress of faith' from the mid-1930s onwards. Graduates from Harvard entered the world of respectable academics, aided by the Institute for Biblical Research, and by publishing companies like Eerdmans with its Bible commentary series. The future looked bright.

FLIRTATION TOWARDS THE TWENTY-FIRST CENTURY

In 1977 J B Phillips, whose paraphrase of the New Testament in English was read by millions, published a book entitled *Ring of Truth*. In it he claimed,

'I should like to make it quite clear that I could not possibly hold the extreme "fundamentalist" position of so-called "verbal inspiration" ... There still survives a minority who passionately believe in verbal inspiration ... Any man who has sense as well as faith is bound to conclude that it is the truths which are inspired and not the words, which are merely the vehicles of truth.' [10]

Many unsuspecting evangelicals considered this to be an excellent book, and Christian bookshops made attractive displays of it. Phillips was, of course, entitled to his opinion and to publish it, but it was completely opposed to the historic evangelical doctrine of Scripture.

---

10 J B Phillips, *Ring of Truth* (Waterbrook Press, Colorado Springs, OH. 2000), p. 15. In 1 Corinthians 14:22 Phillips revised the verse to say what he thought Paul really meant. See Book 4 chapter 5 in this series for more on Phillips.

Similarly, evangelicals were reading and recommending the Bible commentaries by William Barclay who, though frequently expressing a high regard for the Bible as the word of God, had no commitment to inerrancy and felt free to deny the recorded miracles, downgrade Paul's authority and doubt much of the Old Testament history.

The philosophy of Linguistic Analysis was replaced by Logical Positivism which claimed that all statements are open to new interpretations. Modernism, now referred to as 'liberalism', did not feel threatened by the new breed of evangelicals, but welcomed their rich perspectives to add to the ongoing debate about the Bible. Perhaps without realizing it, but certainly to gain credibility with the academic world, many evangelical scholars began to flirt with the new modernism.

The first to notice this shift were the liberal scholars themselves. James Barr, a Scots theologian, and John A T Robinson, a respected New Testament scholar whose book *Honest to God* was a best-seller in the 1960s, rejoiced at the new 'openness' to critical approaches amongst evangelicals. Robinson commented how glad he was to see among evangelicals 'an open and not merely half-hearted acceptance' of critical scholarly disciplines as entirely compatible with the authority of Scripture; this he described as 'a breakthrough'.[11] He was reviewing an evangelical author who had conceded:

'There may be a stage at which the difficulties involved in explaining away an apparent historical error are greater than those caused by accepting the existence of the error ... One may ask whether there is a stage when the number of alleged historical difficulties for which there is yet no solution must lead the conservative scholar to conclude that the absolute historical reliability of the New Testament is a mirage'.[12]

In his strident attack on the evangelical approach to Scripture, James Barr observed what he called a 'liberal evangelicalism'. He drew attention to the *New Bible Commentary* of 1954 and its revision in 1970, and the

---

11 A review in *The Churchman* by John A T Robinson of *New Testament Interpretation* ed. I Howard Marshall (Paternoster Press 1977), p. 55.
12 *New Testament Interpretation* ed. I Howard Marshall. (Paternoster Press 1977).

New Bible Dictionary of 1962 each of which, published by InterVarsity Press, conceded to modern science by allowing a symbolic understanding of Genesis 1.[13] Perceptively, he saw the shift in an evangelical author broadening the definition of inerrancy and allowing the possibility of occasional errors in Scripture whilst still maintaining inerrancy.[14] For all his disgust of the evangelical position on inerrancy—what he called 'a pathological condition of Christianity'—Barr poked uncomfortably (and tediously) at the shift in much of evangelicalism in the mid-twentieth century.

In their flirtation with liberalism, many evangelicals began subtle shifts of terminology. They talked about the Bible as 'infallible' but not 'inerrant', claiming that infallibility refers to the truth of Scripture statements, whilst inerrancy refers to its facts and history; there may be inaccuracies in the second, but never in the first. However, this is a false distinction, and the two words should never be opposed like this. Of the two, infallible is the stronger word but only because it contains inerrancy within it. Something can be inerrant without being infallible, but nothing can be infallible without being inerrant. Occasionally a newspaper report is accurate to the point of being without error, but no one would claim that the article was infallible. The *Oxford English Dictionary* definition of the word 'infallible' begins, 'Incapable of erring'.

Other evangelicals committed themselves to the position that, even if 'minor discrepancies' were to be found in Scripture, this would in no way upset their confidence in the Bible as the word of God. They could write of 'a basic historical core' in the Bible, and the fact that the historical accuracy of some narratives 'should perhaps be held with certain reservations.' Bernard Ramm wrote of the humanity of Scripture in this way: 'We must also have a doctrine of the Scriptures which is of the same heartbeat as the theology of the cross … God's written word … shares the brokenness, the servanthood, the masking of the divine glory

---

13 James Barr, *Fundamentalism* (SCM Press 1977), pp. 26, 41–42.
14 As above with reference to Michael Green, *The Authority of Scripture* (Falcon Books 1963), pp. 29ff.

as the incarnate son…'[15] Thus, he concluded, the Bible has the stamp of man and his fallibility upon it. Professor Ramm overlooked that Christ, with whom he compared the Bible, was both perfectly God and perfectly man and as such was without error or sin.

In a similar fashion, two American theologians, Professors Rogers and McKim, maintained that in the Bible, God accommodated himself to human limitations of understanding when he spoke to us in human language. He never expected us to look to the Bible for accurate detail in historical and scientific statements, but to discover salvation truth in Jesus Christ. They concluded that the writers of the Bible were not interested in detailed accuracy, and the 'small errors' that trouble evangelicals today did not in the slightest bother them; they were not intentionally, or even knowingly, inaccurate, but because of their human weakness they inevitably made mistakes in recording events. The argument concludes that Christ and his salvation message is the authority of the Bible, not its accurate words.[16]

Close to this is the view that some miracles are to be viewed as the misunderstanding of pre-scientific man: 'Some of the cases of demon possession in the Gospels can be demythologized at least to some extent. In particular, Mark 9:14–26 is probably a good example of pre-scientific man attributing to demon possession a malady whose physical mechanism we have since learnt to identify and largely control'—in other words, epilepsy. By way of concession the writers added, 'though not wanting to eliminate the spiritual dimension of this or any illness.'[17] This statement overlooks the fact that the Gospel writer Matthew was careful to make the distinction between 'those oppressed by demons, epileptics and paralytics' (Matthew 4:24 *English Standard Version*).

---

15 A review of Harold Lindsell's, *The Battle for the Bible* (Zondervan, Harper Collins, Nashville TN 1978).

16 Jack B Rogers and Donald K McKim, *The Authority and Interpretation of the Bible: An Historical Approach* (Wipf & Stock Publishers, Eugene OR 1999).

17 James Dunn and Graham Twelftree. 'Demon-Possession and Exorcism in The New Testament', the *Churchman* (1980), p. 222.

Some offered the 'doctrine of intention', suggesting that perhaps the Gospel writers did not intend us to take all that they wrote as historically accurate: 'What if it never was the fourth evangelist's intention that the extended discourses of the fourth gospel should be understood as uttered by Jesus during his ministry on earth?'[18] It is not sufficient to say, 'The Bible is true in the sense in which its authors intended it to be understood as true', in one sense this is correct, but it is not helpful unless explained. According to 1 Peter 1:10–12, some of the Old Testament prophets did not know what was intended by their message, but that is very different from the straightforward historical recording of the Gospel writers.

All was not so bleak in the latter half of the twentieth century. In 1977 the International Council on Biblical Inerrancy was formed in the United States of America under the chairmanship of James Montgomery Boice with a council of sixteen. Concerned at the erosion of a belief in the authority and accuracy of Scripture, the ICBI set out to provide conferences and publications that would explain and defend the conservative evangelical position on inerrancy. In ten years of vigorous work the Council gave hundreds of lectures and published scores of papers and books from the best evangelical scholarship. (See in this series Book 2 chapter 7 for the ICBI statement.)

CONFUSION IN THE TWENTY-FIRST CENTURY

Flirting is at times subtle but always dangerous, and if it is not fully understood it can lead to disaster. To speak of the Bible as trustworthy and reliable 'in those matters which it prescribes as all-important', or 'infallible in all that it affirms', leaves open a wide door of interpretation in what is 'all-important' and what the Bible does and does not 'affirm'. This confusion led the evangelical theologian Francis Schaeffer to refer to the Bible as 'true truth', to make it clear that what the Bible said was all to be taken as reliable. Perhaps without realizing it, evangelicals were accommodating to the language of liberalism. Although Francis Schaeffer

---

18 James Dunn in the *Churchman* in 1982 during a vigorous attack upon the views of Benjamin B Warfield (See Book 2 chapter 2 in this series for Warfield's position).

claimed, over three decades ago: 'Evangelicalism is not consistently evangelical unless there is a line drawn between those who take a full view of Scripture and those who do not',[19] his conclusion is as relevant now as then.

It is unhelpful to read of evangelicals referring to the Bible as the 'nearest' to a final authority that men can find, and to be told that whether or not the story of Jonah and the fish is historical fact is unimportant, because it is the 'divine authoritativeness' of the message that really matters. This is exactly the reasoning of many liberal critics of the Bible who are willing to accept the truth of the Bible but not its accuracy. Karl Barth (1886–1968) was a Swiss theologian-pastor who taught just this. Barth exercised a considerable influence during the first half of the twentieth century. He denied that the Bible is the word of God, but taught that it becomes God's word when it speaks to us. Barth had no interest in discussing whether or not the Bible was without error—he was sure it was not—but he believed its authority did not depend upon its factual trustworthiness. Its authority was not objective (true for everybody everywhere) but subjective (true for anyone when it speaks).

There is a short step from this to the debate about how we should understand the Bible, and this is the issue confronting the twenty-first century. The technical word for this is 'hermeneutics', from the Greek verb 'to interpret'. It has been correctly observed that every theology stands on a hermeneutic; in other words, how you interpret the Bible governs what you believe. Hermeneutics will be discussed in Book 6 chapters 2 and 3 of this series.

Influenced by a new wave of thinking, some have begun to reinterpret the Scriptures whilst often vigorously maintaining a loyalty to its trustworthiness. There are at least five significant influences in the twenty-first century, although they began long before this.

• Post-modernism is the new clothes for existentialism. In brief, it means that all authoritarian and dogmatic statements are disallowed. The only thing we can be certain about is that nothing is certain.

---

19 Francis Schaeffer, *The Great Evangelical Disaster* (Crossway, Wheaton II 1984), p. 51.

- A second influence, which flows from the first, is that of pluralism: the view that all opinions—and this includes religious opinions—are equally valid or not, and none is to be advanced above others.

- Total equality (the word used is egalitarianism), reveals itself particularly in the feminist debate and extreme gender neutral translations. (See Book 4 chapter 5 in this series).

- A pressure, though hardly a philosophy, is that of 'political correctness'. The need to keep within the law by guarding what we say and how we say it has become an increasingly controversial issue today.

- The scientism of evolution—a commitment to a theory that has little basis in observational science—has compelled many evangelicals to adjust their understanding of the creation account. They will rightly warn Christians not to be lured by the moral world-view of twenty-first century society, yet allow themselves to be captured by its false science.

On a whole range of issues, many professing to be evangelical Christians have shifted from the traditional ground under the pressure of these influences, and it means that whilst retaining a belief in the full authority and inerrancy of the Bible, it is possible to deny fundamental truths of doctrine and practice that had rarely been challenged in evangelical life for centuries.

Never, in its long and honourable history, has the evangelical position been so fragmented and confused as it is in the opening decades of the twenty-first century. The doctrines of creation, gender, sexuality and marriage, hell, the omniscience of God, the value of Old Testament law, justification by faith, the propitiatory death of Christ, and Christ as the only way of salvation, are currently in open debate among many who profess a 'high view of Scripture'. This inevitably influences moral issues once never questioned among evangelicals. This stems from a shaky view of the absolute inerrancy of Scripture or a poor understanding of how to interpret it.

Scholarship and criticism

It may be helpful to define some terms used in the academic world of biblical studies. They are included here simply to illustrate how wide is the world of Bible criticism, and to acquaint those who wish to be 'in the know' with some of the current issues discussed among Bible scholars. Not all of these approaches are unhelpful—some of them are indispensable to our understanding of Scripture; but all of them can become destructive if used without care and attention. The following descriptions are brief and therefore inadequate to fully describe what are often detailed academic discussions; this is merely a simple introduction to each.

TEXTUAL CRITICISM

Textual Criticism, or 'Lower Criticism', is the study of the texts of the manuscripts and documents of the Bible to discover the best and most accurate text for the Bible. See Book 4 chapter 4 in this series. This is unavoidable and indispensable in the study of the Bible.

LITERARY CRITICISM

Literary Criticism, or 'Higher Criticism' as it is more commonly called, builds on the results of Textual Criticism (thus it is 'higher') and is the study of the way the Bible stories have been put together and how reliable the claims and stories really are. It is concerned with the structure, date and authorship of the books of the Bible, and the literary style (whether it is history, poetry and so on).

Higher Criticism is a phrase that was first used by the German scholar J G Eichhorn in the preface to his second edition of *Old Testament Studies* in 1787. Eichhorn rejected the reliability of the Old Testament. Even before Eichhorn, in 1753 the French physician Jean Astruc suggested the idea that Genesis was compiled from two sources, one using the name *Jahweh* (Jehovah) for God and the other using the word *Elohim*. This view was taken up and expanded by Julius Wellhausen as we saw above. The term Higher Criticism does not necessarily imply a liberal criticism of the Bible, but since in practice it almost always has done, it is commonly used to refer to those who deny the trustworthiness of

Scripture. Some of the following 'criticisms' can be seen as subdivisions of Literary Criticism.

SOURCE CRITICISM

Source Criticism is the study of the material that supposedly lies behind the Bible stories. It asks where the writers obtained their material, how much of it is original and how much is borrowed from other sources—did they obtain it from oral or written accounts? The discussion about which of our four Gospels was written first, who borrowed what from whom, and whether there is a mysterious source known as 'Q' (see in this series Book 3 chapter 6), is all part of Source Criticism.

There is value in a proper use of Source Criticism to understand the contemporary world of the biblical writers, but its danger has been in the readiness of critics to deny the claimed authorship of the Bible books and also to assume that the writers merely copied ideas from other religions and cultures. Thus, Moses formed his laws from the Hammurabi Codes, the Jews borrowed their ceremonies from surrounding nations, the prophets copied their visions from contemporary culture, and so on. This denies the unique authority of God's revelation in the Bible. One of the first areas of debate by the Source Critics was the first five books of the Bible. As we saw earlier it was suggested that these books were compiled by various editors known as J, E, P and D, depending on whether a passage contained the divine name *Jahweh* (J), the normal word *Elohim* for God (E), or whether it contained priestly information about sacrifice and ceremonies (P) or the laws of Deuteronomy (D). Inevitably the critics rarely agreed with each other.

FORM CRITICISM

Form Criticism builds on all this and asks why the stories are in the form they are, and in what form they were passed on before being committed to writing. The Form Critic wants to know what the original story was, before all the bits and pieces of the story-tellers' imagination or bias was added. For example, if a liberal Form Critic assumes that the Gospels were written in the second century there will be an attempt to discover, in the form of the writings, whether we can identify the actual words Jesus may have uttered. One of the tests the Form Critics use is that of 'dissimilarity'; this assumes that if a statement in the Gospels is unlike anything we expect of the second century church, and unlike anything the Jews taught, then it might be the actual words of Jesus.

Rudolf Bultmann, a professor at the University of Marburg in Germany before his death in 1976, used Form Criticism in a devastating way in the New Testament. Bultmann was an 'expert' in demythologizing, and assumed that all we have in the Gospels is the Jesus of the wishful imagination of the second or third century church as stories were passed from generation to generation. In his book *Jesus and the Word*, Bultmann concluded, 'We can know almost nothing about the life and personality of Jesus.' However, what mattered was the Christ of faith, not the Jesus of history. This approach was followed more recently by The Jesus Seminar led by Robert Funk before his death in 2005. Their conclusion is that we can know almost nothing of what Jesus really said.[20]

REDACTION CRITICISM

Redaction Criticism refers to the various editors (redactors) who compiled Scripture and arranged the material to suit their theme. For example, Bultmann believed the second century church invented and altered stories in order to portray their concept of Christ; for an Old Testament critic, it might be post-exilic priests tampering with old stories of the origins of primitive tribes to produce a glorious history of Israel.

In a more restricted and positive sense, all who examine the Bible carefully engage in redaction criticism when they consider how the Gospel writers, for example, adapted their material to suit their theme. Matthew and Luke differ from each other in the precise order of the last two temptations of Christ; one response is that since neither claims to present an exact order, each is free to close with the temptation best suited to his

---

20 The Jesus Seminar published a series of books including: The Five Gospels: *The Search for the Authentic Words of Jesus* (1993), *The Acts of Jesus: The Search for the Authentic Deeds of Jesus* (1998). With the death of Funk, it morphed into the Jesus Project and continues its studies today.

theme—Matthew presenting Christ as King, and Luke presenting him as Man. This is engaging in Redaction Criticism.

However, a more liberal approach to Redaction Criticism assumes that those who copied the original texts changed, or even invented, details to fit their theological purpose. In the hands of unwary evangelicals, Redaction Criticism has allowed them to assume that the Gospel writers, for example, have tampered with facts to highlight their theology.[21]

HISTORICAL CRITICISM

There are two parts to Historical Criticism. The first is the need to understand the Bible in its original historical context; it is important to appreciate the culture and customs of the age in which the Biblical writer lived. All who read the Bible appreciate help in this way.

However, it is assumed among some scholars that in their records the ancients paid little attention to accuracy. As one evangelical writer has expressed it: 'None of the documents which make up the New Testament would pass as history in the modern sense. Edward Gibbon and Leopold von Ranke were not about at the time to write it.'[22] We may therefore discover where the biblical writers sat loosely to historical accuracy to fit their purpose. But this argument is based on an unsound foundation. Both Gibbon and von Ranke are hardly models for unprejudiced and wholly reliable reporting since both were strongly biased in their assessment of history.

Besides, there were some first-rate historians in the ancient world who placed a high premium on accuracy. Among Greek writers, Herodotus, who lived about the same time as Ezra and Nehemiah, allowed some freedom in reporting speeches, but not in narratives.

In the second century AD Lucian of Samosata, writing to Philo, demanded that 'History abhors the intrusion of any least scruple of falsehood ... The historian's one task is to tell the thing as it happened

21 For a discussion of the history and pros and cons of Redaction Criticism see *Foundations* Issue no. 4, May 1980, 'Redaction Criticism and the Evangelical drift' by Brian Edwards. Accessed from the Affinity website archives.
22 Bruce Chilton in *Themelios*, April 1978.

… Facts are not to be collected haphazard, but with careful, laborious, repeated investigation; when possible, a man should have been present and seen for himself…'[23] Lucian referred to Thucydides in the fifth century BC as one who gives us the model. Thucydides was not always able to give the speeches he heard word for word, but he did claim to adhere 'as closely as possible to the general sense of what was actually spoken.'

Above all this, we should not forget that an evangelical understanding of Scripture is that it is 'God-breathed' under the superintendence of the Holy Spirit (2 Timothy 3:16 and 2 Peter 1:21). See Book 2 chapter 2 in this series.

CANONICAL CRITICISM

The word 'canon' means a rule or standard, and Canonical Criticism is interested not so much in the material that makes up the contents of the books of the Bible (Source and Form Criticism), but in the reasons why the completed books were accepted as authoritative in the life of the Old Testament or New Testament church and the effect this had upon the community. It considers how the community shaped what was accepted, or why it rejected it. Books of the Bible must be studied as a whole and their value seen as the authoritative Scripture of a believing community. It is a relatively new study, placing less emphasis on the form, structure and redaction, but accepting the books of the Bible as complete and considering their influence that shaped the Old and New covenant life. It often pleases neither liberals nor conservatives.[24]

See Book 3 in this series for the canon of the Bible which is a different subject.

THE NEW HERMENEUTIC

The word 'hermeneutic' refers to our way of interpreting Scripture. Again, this is an important study. See Book 6 chapters 2 and 3 of this series for how we should understand the Bible. However, the New Hermeneutic

---

23 Lucian 'The way to write History' chs. 7, 38, 47.
24 Canon Criticism is new into the field of biblical discussion and is seen in Brevard Childs, *Introduction to the Old Testament as Scripture* (Augsburg Fortress, Minneapolis MN), 1959.

is different. It is especially concerned with the way the Bible 'speaks' to a modern reader. The New Hermeneutic sees every application of the text of the Bible as an event to be experienced by the modern reader or listener. The study of form, structure, source and redaction is helpful, but that may leave us with a dry and sterile book that merely relates things about history. We must somehow make every act of interpreting Scripture a living experience.

The New Hermeneutic assumes that for the dynamic relationship between the text and the interpreter to be meaningful, there may be many meanings of the text, each different according to the identity and situation of those interpreting it. We therefore cannot expect to find one universal meaning for a passage of Scripture. There is some truth in this, since the same passage, correctly understood in its context, can be applied to many situations. However, the effect of the New Hermeneutic can be that ultimately a reader may make the Bible say anything that appeals to them and there is no final and correct understanding of any text; anyone can 'hear' the Bible say anything.

According to the New Hermeneutic we are not looking for the meaning of the words or statements in the Bible so much as their effect upon us. That is not the evangelical view of Scripture, because it confuses the clear voice of the authority of God that we find in his word. Truth is not what we make it, but what God revealed. There is a failure in the New Hermeneutic to appreciate that much contained in the New Testament letters is there to establish a precise, and not a fluid, understanding of Christian theology.[25]

CONTEXTUALIZATION

For all its length, the word sums up a very simple issue facing the church today and we can summarize it like this: how do we convey what God has said in his word through men who lived in an ancient culture, to those who live in a very different culture, via translators or preachers who live in a culture that is different from the other two? There are therefore at least

---

25 A detailed critique of Ernst Fuchs and Gerhard Ebeling can be found on line by Anthony C Thiselton, *Gospel Studies*, 'The new hermeneutic'.

three cultures involved. Making a faithful and meaningful 'tri-cultural' communication of biblical truth is an issue of great importance today.

Contextualising is employed whenever a teacher explains the significance of, for example, a Greek word in its first century context or an event in its Old Testament context. The danger is to avoid the hard work that is needed to communicate the text faithfully to another culture rather than allow a contemporary culture to dictate how we understand the Bible. This has led to a number of distortions: for example, a 'prosperity gospel', which makes the word of God say what a capitalist society wants it to say, or a 'black theology', which takes the Bible as a charter for positive discrimination, and the 'theology of liberation' which forces the Bible to give support to active terrorism simply because the oppression and corruption in a particular culture seem to call for this. We are all in danger of making the Bible say what our culture wants it to say, and that is an abuse of contextualization.

2. Great minds on a great book

The conclusions of many brilliant scholars has repeatedly shown that confidence in the complete accuracy of the biblical record is perfectly consistent with a thinking mind.

Evangelical Christianity believes in the truth and historical accuracy of the Bible in all its statements, and that this is what Jesus and the apostles clearly taught (see Book 2 in this series). The challenge of many critics to the evangelical position is that to believe that the Bible is God's errorless word and that it contains within its pages nothing but the truth, is simply an unthinking position which is impossible to maintain if we have 'sense as well as faith.' [26] Admittedly there are problems and difficulties of 'apparent' contradictions and errors, and these will be dealt with in later chapters, but the purpose here is to establish that true scholarship supports the accuracy of the biblical records.

The force of truth

Writing in *The Babylonians*, the author concludes, 'Without question the biblical story of Noah and the Flood rests on a Babylonian prototype from the beginning of the second millennium BC'.[27] Robert Funk, who led the Jesus Seminar researching into how much of the Gospels can really be attributed to Jesus, affirmed: 'New Testament scholars have established beyond any reasonable doubt that the Jesus of the early Christian documents is to some extent a figment of the Christian imagination.' [28] Those phrases *without question* and *beyond any reasonable doubt*, are designed to prevent any further discussion.

---

26 A conclusion by J B Phillips in *Ring of Truth*.
27 H W E Sagg, *The Babylonians* (The London Folio Society, 1999), p. 412.
28 *The Five Gospels* (Harper. San Francisco 1998).

JOHN A T ROBINSON—'THE TYRANNY OF UNEXAMINED ASSUMPTIONS'

In 1976 John A T Robinson, Dean at Trinity College, Cambridge, and recognised as a first-class New Testament scholar, published a book called, *Redating the New Testament*.[29] The book sent shock waves through the academic world of New Testament criticism. Although, as a liberal and critical scholar, Robinson began his work as a 'theological joke', the evidence increasingly compelled him to take his own results more seriously. He finally concluded that the entire New Testament had been completed before AD 70. It is certainly a work of detailed scholarship in which every New Testament book is carefully examined.

Robinson early discovered in his research that the greatest argument for an early date of the Gospels and epistles was the total absence of the 'single most datable and climactic event of the period—the fall of Jerusalem in AD 70'. In this year, the besieging Roman army finally broke into the city, massacred its defenders and destroyed the Temple. This would have been a conclusive vindication for the New Testament writers that God had finished with the 'types and shadows' of the Jewish ceremonial law—yet not one of the Gospels or letters refers to the destruction of the Temple as already completed. Robinson concluded that the only satisfactory reason for this silence was that the event had not yet taken place. A conclusion unusual for a liberal critic, but one which evangelicals had never doubted.

One main reason why most critical scholars placed the Gospels after AD 70 was because these documents contained prophecies concerning the destruction of Jerusalem, and the phenomena of prophecy could not be allowed. Elsewhere, Robinson wisely considered that it was a reasonable working assumption that the Acts of the Apostles could be trusted until proved otherwise. He concluded that the 'majority of English scholars' accept Luke's authorship of Acts.[30] Robinson was compelled to admit that, 'There would seem to be a detectable swing back, if not to apostolic authorship [of the pastoral epistles] at any rate to taking seriously' the

---

29 John A T Robinson, *Redating the New Testament* (SCM Press, London 1976).
30 *Redating the New Testament*, pp. 85, 86.

possibility of their being penned in the lifetime of Paul.[31] That, of course, leaves us with the amusing possibility that the letters claiming to come from Paul were written within his lifetime, without his knowledge, by person or persons unknown, whilst the great apostle himself has left us not a word to his credit!

Equally as 'shocking' as the conclusions Robinson came to regarding the completion of the New Testament books, are his comments about so much modern scholarship. John Robinson was a liberal critic who, to the day of his death in 1983, remained a liberal in his view of the authorship and accuracy of the New Testament books. Robinson commented: 'Datings that seem agreed in the textbooks can suddenly appear much less secure than the consensus would suggest.'[32] Elsewhere he claimed, 'It is astonishing that so much has continued to be built upon so little.'[33] And again: 'It is sobering too to discover how little basis there is for many of the dates confidently assigned by modern experts to the New Testament documents.'[34] He wrote of 'circular arguments' and 'presuppositions' and deplored what he called, 'disconcertingly tenuous deductions', 'sheer scholarly laziness' and 'the tyranny of unexamined assumptions'.[35] Perhaps the most damning comment is Robinson's perception of 'almost wilful blindness' and 'the consistent evasion by modern commentators of a solution they have already prejudged to be impossible.'[36]

These devastating comments are paralleled by the assessment of an unrivalled scholar six decades earlier, William Mitchell Ramsay (see below), who wrote of the 'fallacy, ignorance and pretentiousness of the critics.'[37]

---

31 As above, p. 70.
32 As above, p. 1.
33 As above, p. 229.
34 As above, p. 341.
35 As above, pp. 9, 341, 345.
36 As above, p. 342.
37 William Mitchell Ramsay, *The Bearing of Recent Discovery on the Trustworthiness of the New Testament*, p. 227. A series of lectures given at Union Theological Seminary, Virginia in 1913.

ETA LINNEMANN—'I HAD MISLED MY STUDENTS'

In 1990 Eta Linnemann published a book called *Historical Criticism of the Bible: Methodology or Ideology?* [38] Such a title would not normally attract the attention of any except those dedicated to academic theology, but in this case the book was of unusual interest and it was the subtitle that was shocking: 'Reflections of a Bultmannian turned Evangelical.' Eta Linnemann (1926–2009), as the popular Professor of New Testament in the Philipps University at Marburg in Germany, had written a number of bestselling books in which she destroyed the confidence of her readers in the Bible as the inerrant word of God. It was her conviction that the Bible was inaccurate as a book about history and unreliable as a book about God and that it was her mission to prove this.

Slowly, however, the professor at Marburg and dedicated student of Rudolf Bultmann, Ernst Fuchs and Gerhard Eberling, became disillusioned with her own method of study. She confessed, 'I became aware of what folly it is to maintain that the miracles of the New Testament never took place … It was clear to me that my teaching was a case of the blind leading the blind. I repented for the way I had misled my students.' In this latest book, Eta Linnemann regarded everything she has ever taught and written as rubbish. She admitted that she had thrown some of her most popular and critical books into the bin and advised her readers: 'I ask you sincerely to do the same thing with any of them you have on your own bookshelves.' In her case the force of truth had triumphed.

TWO OUTSTANDING SCHOLARS

During the past century and into a new millennium, many scholars have come to the defence of the historical accuracy of the Bible with learning and skill. Unfortunately, they are frequently ignored because we are all in danger of ignoring those whose positions we cannot answer. Two are considered in this chapter. One represents the Old Testament and the other the New Testament.

---

38 Eta Linnemann, *Historical Criticism of the Bible: Methodology or Ideology? Reflections of a Bultmannian Turned Evangelical.* Trans. Robert W Yarbrough (Baker, Grand Rapids MI 1990).

These two men were acknowledged to be leading experts and scholars with first-class minds. There was nothing casual or lazy about their methods of study. They were men searching for truth. They each began at a different starting point—one committed to the inerrancy of the Bible and the other not—yet both arrived at the same conclusion. Their work has been added to in recent years as new discoveries have been made, but nothing has yet been discovered that alters their general conclusion regarding the complete accuracy of the Bible. They can still be referred to with confidence.

Professor Robert Dick Wilson (1856–1930)

Early in the twentieth century, it was assumed that evangelicals, like a tiny David, were being overwhelmed by the Goliaths in the universities. Professors Ewald and Wellhausen, at Göttingen in Germany, and Driver and Gray, at Oxford in England, were names that stood for great scholarship, brilliant intellect and careful research. Between them, they denied the accuracy of the Bible, and their views, though altered by modern critics, still form the basis of arguments against its inerrancy.

Robert Dick Wilson was Professor of Semitic Philology (the languages and literature of the Middle East) at Princeton Theological Seminary in the United States of America, during the 1920s. In 1929 he left Princeton with others to form the Westminster Theological Seminary. Wilson's scholarship, though little spoken of today, excelled that of the learning of the great critics at Göttingen and Oxford. He was born in 1856 and during his student days in Germany, Wilson worked out a programme for his life. He planned to spend fifteen years in language study, fifteen more in the study of the Old Testament text in the light of these languages and, finally, fifteen years in publishing his findings. Those first fifteen years were remarkable.

Wilson learned a few languages by filling the odd moments of time: Greek, Latin, French, German, Hebrew, Italian, Spanish, Portuguese, biblical Aramaic, Syriac, Arabic—and a few more. Wilson then moved to Heidelberg in Germany to study Babylonian. To these he added Ethiopic, Phoenician, all the Aramaic dialects, Egyptian, Coptic, Persian and Armenian. These were the 'semitic' languages. During those first fifteen years Robert Dick Wilson became familiar with some twenty-six languages and dialects; many of these he studied under the leading professors of his day. Throughout the following fifteen years, Wilson collected over 100,000 quotations from these languages to illustrate basic facts proving the accuracy of Scripture.

When Wilson responded to the arguments and questioned the scholarship of the 'higher critics', he did so from a greater height than they themselves had attained. His conclusions have not been negated by more recent research. Footnotes refer to contemporary scholars who are recognised in their fields and whose conclusions support those of Robert Dick Wilson.

ABRAHAM'S EXPEDITION IN GENESIS 14

The German critic Wellhausen read the account of the raid of Chedorlaomer against the Kings of Sodom and Gomorrah and his subsequent defeat by Abraham (Genesis 14), and for various reasons concluded these accounts 'are simply impossibilities'. Wilson showed that such expeditions were not uncommon at that time and that the names given to the kings in the Bible account are also found in literature of the surrounding nations.[39] Without any evidence, the critics could only claim that an unknown Jewish writer, somewhere between 900 and 300 BC, had invented the story in honour of Abraham by using names he had discovered.

This instance is so typical of the critical approach to Scripture and Wilson's response, that we should have his own words:

'Against the historical character of this narrative we have the assertion of Wellhausen and other critics of our times (only about 4,000 years after the supposed expedition!) that the expedition was "simply impossible", and that it is probable that the account may have been fabricated (or forged) by some person unknown, at some time unknown, for reasons unknown. Not one item of evidence in the way of

---

39 K A Kitchen, an acknowledged Old Testament scholar and archaeologist offers the same evidence for this section: *On the Reliability of the Old Testament* (Eerdmans Publishing Company, Grand Rapids and Cambridge 2003), pp. 319–323.

time, place, logic, psychology, language, or customs, has been produced against the trustworthiness of the document … But a German professor says it is "simply impossible", English followers echo "simply impossible", and the Americans echo again "simply impossible". And this assertion of "simply impossible" is called an "assured result of scientific criticism"!' [40]

In the years of Robert Dick Wilson's research, it was common for critical scholars to deny Moses as the author of the first five books and that Abraham was a real person—he was no more than a legendary hero. Every argument put forward by the critics was shown by Wilson to be totally without foundation.

THE DATE OF EZRA, NEHEMIAH AND CHRONICLES

Critics generally demand a late date (around 300 BC) for these three books, partly because they use an expression 'King of Persia' in a form which, it was claimed, was 'unnecessary and contrary to all contemporary usage.' In response, Wilson gathered quotations and references, particularly from Babylonian, Persian, Susian and Egyptian sources, showing that from 400 BC down to Caesar Augustus in AD 14:

'It was the custom in all times, languages, and kingdoms, to use titles similar to this', and that this exact title was used by Nabunaid [Nabonidus] of Babylon to refer to Cyrus in 546 BC—seven years before its first use in the Bible. Wilson revealed that this title—so 'contrary to all contemporary usage'—was employed thirty-eight times, by eighteen authors, representing six languages, between 546 and 365 BC. [41]

Why, asked the evangelical, had not the learned professors read these sources for themselves? Then Wilson challenged the infallibility of Ewald, Wellhausen, Driver and Gray: 'Having read carefully and repeatedly what these critics have to say on this title, I have failed to find any hint indicating that they have ever appealed for their information to any original sources

---

40 Robert Dick Wilson, *A Scientific Investigation of the Old Testament* (Marshall Brothers Ltd, London and Edinburgh 1926), p. 22.
41 Edwin M Yamauchi offers additional evidence for the biblical date of these books, *Persia and the Bible* (Baker Books. Grand Rapids 1990), pp. 381–394.

outside of Greek, Hebrew and Aramaic.' Perhaps this was because they could not easily read beyond these three.

THE ACCURACY OF THE OLD TESTAMENT COPYISTS

In Book 4 chapter 2 of this series, the care of copyists was considered. Robert Dick Wilson illustrated the careful accuracy of the Old Testament in the following way. Twenty-six foreign kings are referred to in the Hebrew Old Testament, and in all but three instances the spelling is virtually identical with that found in inscriptions made by these kings themselves. Over many centuries the names were copied with unswerving accuracy to the extent that the one hundred and twenty consonants involved in these names are all in exactly the right order.[42]

In contrast to this biblical accuracy, an Egyptian priest (Manetho) wrote a history of Egyptian dynasties (*Aegyptiaca*) somewhere around the year 280 BC. He includes one hundred and forty names of kings of Egypt and only forty-nine are clearly recognizable when compared with the relevant monuments and inscriptions. Ptolemy, the mathematician, astronomer and geographer of the second century AD, whose conclusions were accepted without question for thirteen centuries, listed eighteen kings of Babylon and most of these bear no resemblance to the names on monuments and inscriptions.

There are more than forty kings of Israel and Judah referred to in the Bible. Each is found in the correct order and references to the kings of surrounding nations are all accurate when checked with the records of those nations. By any fair critic, the Bible must be seen to be an amazingly accurate book. If there is such care over the spelling and order of names, is it not reasonable to expect a similar care in recording the words and actions of these kings?

THE USE OF FOREIGN WORDS AND CUSTOMS IN THE OLD TESTAMENT

In any collection of documents written over a long period of time, we would expect to find the use of foreign words reflecting the influence of

---

42 See K A Kitchen above for the same conclusion, p. 62.

the nation that held world power at that time. This would confirm the date and order of the documents, for it would be almost impossible for an author of a later date to insert words and customs unfamiliar to him. For example, it would be impossible for a present-day author to write a novel based upon a family who lived five hundred years ago, unless he had first undertaken a significant amount of historical research to ensure that the words and customs were exact.

Wilson demonstrated that the customs and words used in the Old Testament reveal each book to have been written at the time it claims to have been written; we find foreign words in the Old Testament just where we would expect to find them. The early chapters of Genesis contain a number of Babylonian words. Later in Genesis, Egyptian words are introduced. Solomon's writing contains Indian and Assyrian words. During the period of the kings of Judah and Israel, there is a return of Assyrian and Babylonian terms. Daniel, Ezra, Nehemiah, Esther and Chronicles all contain a number of Persian words used for the first time in the Bible. There is strong evidence that during the time of Jeremiah and the exile, Aramaic was the common language of Western Asia and the business language of the Jews. This would explain why one verse in Jeremiah and half of Ezra and Daniel are written in Aramaic and not in Hebrew. All these books, therefore, reflect the ruling nation of the day and the area of the world in which the story of the Jews is set.

Significantly also, Wilson showed that Greek words are virtually absent in the Old Testament because by the close of the Old Testament (around 400 BC) Greek power was not yet evident. If, as the higher critics demand, much of the Old Testament was written as late as the second century BC—and some claim Daniel was written in Palestine in 164 BC—where are all the Greek words? There are references to Greek musical instruments, but that is because, as we now know, Nebuchadnezzar the king of Babylon, employed Greek mercenaries in his army.[43]

Some critics also claim that parts of the Pentateuch (Genesis to Deuteronomy), and especially the priestly laws in Leviticus, were not

---

43 See Edwin M Yamauchi in *Persia and the Bible*, pp. 237, 379–394.

written by Moses fifteen hundred years before Christ, but by Ezra and his editors between 500 and 300 BC. This was in the middle of the Persian period and naturally the book of Ezra abounds with Persian words. But there is not one Persian word in those so-called 'priestly documents' in Leviticus. Ezra must have been a quite remarkable forger if he really was writing Leviticus between 500 and 300 BC, to have included Persian words in his own book but carefully excluded them all in the Pentateuch. A more likely conclusion is that the higher critics were wrong.

Robert Dick Wilson maintained that each narrative and section of the Old Testament reveals the customs of that particular time which would have been unknown to writers a few centuries later. Among the many examples, is the fact that the reference to the horse appears first in the story of Joseph at the very time we know the horse was being introduced into Western Asia and Egypt. On the other hand, Wilson questioned, if so much of the Old Testament was supposed to have been written late in the Greek period, why is there not one reference to the elephant which was, by the time of Greek power, important for both work and war?

It seems that the very least we must claim for these deceivers, who were supposed to have written books of the Bible and then claimed a great age for them, is that the brilliance of their scholarship, their knowledge of history and their literary ability, demanded divine aid not far different from an evangelical view of inspiration!

Critics have also concluded that the understanding of God's character which is found in the earlier parts of the Old Testament—as Creator, Preserver, Guide, Judge, Saviour and Sanctifier—is so far in advance of the beliefs of surrounding nations that the records must have a very late date for their origin. It is true that many ideas about God, man and salvation in the Old Testament are nowhere exactly paralleled in the surrounding nations, but why is this evidence that the books are of a late date? The same evidence might well be argued as a strong case for revelation.

GRAMMAR

Perhaps the very word frightens us away from this subject! How can we compete when Hebrew scholars claim certain terms prove a late date for, say, the book of Ecclesiastes? Professor Delitzsch was one of the finest Hebrew scholars in the nineteenth century, and although he died in 1890, he was a founder of modern Bible criticism. Delitzsch claimed that certain forms in words in Ecclesiastes, like *ûth*, *ôn*, and *ân*, were proof 'beyond all doubt' that this book was not written by Solomon but during the days of Ezra/Nehemiah at the earliest. The German theologian Carl Heinrich Cornill (1854–1920) in his *Introduction to the Canonical Books of the Old Testament* claimed this to be 'absolutely convincing and irrefutable'.[44] But Cornill was only copying Delitzsch.

Wilson had read and studied more widely even than Delitzsch, and could assure us that this great master was mistaken. Wilson noted that in the fifty years since the death of Delitzsch, knowledge of the Hebrew language had moved on greatly. Wilson put forward sixty-seven uses of *ûth* from eight sources between 2,000 and 625 BC; he claimed that this form is found in every book of the Old Testament except Song of Solomon, Ruth and Lamentations—many of them in passages that even the critics themselves allow are early in date. He dealt similarly with *ôn* and *ân*.[45] We may not understand the issues to appreciate the result. True scholarship frequently undermines the 'certainties' of critics. There is no need for us to be cowed by arguments from grammar and syntax; Wilson assured his readers: 'These forms and constructions are irrelevant as evidence of the time at which a document was written.'

WILSON'S CONCLUSIONS

It is impossible in a short space to do justice to the clear arguments of Professor Wilson. Of course, there is much scholarship that has added to the subject since his death in 1930, but nothing to challenge his overall conclusion. His brilliance was unequalled and we are fully justified in accepting his conclusions even when we cannot follow all his arguments; after all, the critics have relied upon such submission to their views for more than a century and a half.

---

44 Carl Heinrich Cornill, *Introduction to the Canonical books of the Old Testament* (Williams and Norgate, London, 1907), p. 449.
45 Robert Dick Wilson, *A Scientific Investigation of the Old Testament*, pp. 105–110.

On the prophets, Wilson commented:

'No one knows enough to affirm with confidence that any one of the prophetic books was not written by the man whose name it bears. No one knows enough to assert that the kings and others mentioned did not do and say what is ascribed to them.'[46]

Wilson complained at what he called the 'inquisitorial' methods of the Old Testament critics; that is, they would assume the Bible to be untrustworthy and misleading, and all evidence challenging this assumption was scorned. This unjustified assumption is still with us. Many critics have ceased to bother whether or not the Bible records are reliable, they simply assume they are not. It is the 'tyranny of unexamined assumptions' that J A T Robinson complained of.

Illustrating the contradictions of many critical conclusions, Wilson commented that they often claim that the presence of Aramaic words indicates a late date of composition, but when books they consider early contain Aramaic words they conclude that they were inserted later: 'Such procedure is contrary to all the laws of evidence, fairness, and common sense.'[47]

Wilson made the reasonable observation that the Old Testament text, as with any piece of historical writing, has the right to be accepted unless or until it is proved false. Reliability in matters of history are a clear indicator of reliability in matters of theology.

Wilson asserted that the Old Testament has a right to be accepted 'until it shall have been proved false', and proof, the Professor sternly demanded, is not the same as the 'opinions of men of our generation.' For too long Christians have been afraid to trust the very words of Scripture in case they find themselves ridiculed by 'scholars'. Professor Wilson had shown that these minds are not always clever, scholarly, or even honest.

Three biblical scholars of the twenty-first century, Kenneth Kitchen and James Hoffmeier (Professors of Egyptology), and Alan Millard (Professor of Assyriology), each urge scholars at least to treat the Bible in the same

---

46 Wilson, *Is the Higher Criticism Scholarly?* (Marshall Brothers Ltd, London and Edinburgh 1922), p. 58.
47 Above, p. 31.

way that they treat other ancient documents, instead of assuming the Bible must be in error until it is proved to be true.

Wilson offered the fruit of his lifetime of painstaking research with the assertion:

'I try to give my students such an intelligent faith in the Old Testament Scriptures, that they will never doubt them as long as they live. I try to give them evidence. I try to show them that there is a reasonable ground for belief in the history of the Old Testament. ... I have now come to the conviction that no man knows enough to assail the truthfulness of the Old Testament[48]... We are scientifically certain that we have substantially the same text that was in the possession of Christ and the apostles and, so far as anybody knows, the same as that written by the original composers of the Old Testament documents.'[49]

Nothing available since his death, including the discovery of the Dead Sea Scrolls, contradicts that. See in this series Book 1 chapter 6 for more on the authentic accuracy of the Old Testament narratives.

Sir William Mitchell Ramsay (1851–1939)

William Ramsay was born in Glasgow, Scotland, and by his death in 1939 he had become the foremost authority of his day on the history of Asia Minor (the land of the Acts of the Apostles, modern Turkey), and a leading scholar in the study of the New Testament. From the post of Professor of Classical Art and Architecture at Oxford, he was appointed Regius Professor of Humanity (the Latin Professorship) at Aberdeen. Knighted in 1906 to mark his distinguished service to the world of scholarship, Ramsay also gained three honorary fellowships from Oxford colleges, nine honorary doctorates from British, Continental and North American universities and became an honorary member of almost every association devoted to archaeology and historical research. He was one of the original members of the British Academy, was awarded the Gold Medal of Pope Leo XIII in 1893 and the Victorian Medal of the Royal Geographical

---

48 Robert Dick Wilson, *Is the Higher Criticism Scholarly?* 1922, pp. 9–10.
49 See also Wilson, *A Scientific Investigation of the Old Testament*, p. 8.

Society in 1906. So many books and articles came from the pen of Sir William Ramsay that it is difficult to obtain a complete list.

Ramsay, unlike Wilson, never claimed to be an evangelical Christian, nor did he commit himself to a view of Bible inerrancy. Significantly, when he began his research he had no interest in proving the accuracy of the New Testament. In 1868, Ramsay had earned the first three prizes in Greek and Latin from his class at the University of Aberdeen and by 1872 he won a five-year scholarship at Oxford. He soon became a keen follower of the professors at Tübingen and Göttingen, fell under the influence of the liberal theologian Ferdinand Christian Baur and in his own words 'worshipped Wellhausen'.

Admitting all this, Ramsay agreed that he 'dutifully accepted the current opinion that the Acts of the Apostles was written during the second half of the second century by an author who wished to influence the minds of people in his own time by a highly wrought and imaginative description of the early church.' Like most Tübingen scholars, he considered that the author of Acts wrote somewhere between the years AD 160–180, cared little for facts of history, or geography, and aimed only to influence the minds of his readers by imaginative stories of his heroes, especially Peter and Paul.[50]

When William Ramsay first went to Asia Minor, many of the cities mentioned in Acts had no known location and almost nothing was known of their detailed history or politics. The Acts of the Apostles was virtually our only record, and Ramsay fully expected his own research to prove the author of Acts hopelessly inaccurate, since no man could possibly know the details of Asia Minor more than a hundred years after the event. He devoted his life to unearthing the ancient cities and documents of Asia Minor and the facts he discovered brought about a fundamental change in his thinking.

In the first place, Ramsay recognized that 'No other ancient traveller has left an account of the journeys which he made across Asia Minor.'

---

50 William Mitchell Ramsay, *The Bearing of Recent Discovery on the Trustworthiness of the New Testament*. First published 1914, pp. 16, 37–38.

Therefore, the account of Luke, if we assume the traditional view of Luke as the author of Acts, had first to be shown to be true or false. If it was proved to be the accurate narrative of an eyewitness then, for Ramsay the historian, it was the most valuable document we were ever likely to possess describing Asia Minor in the first century AD.

Ramsay therefore put the writer of Acts on trial. As noted, Ramsay was an outstanding scholar whose work has still not been surpassed, and he certainly had no preconceived purpose to prove Luke an accurate historian—quite the reverse. After a lifetime of study, however, this was his conclusion:

'Further study of Acts 13 to 21 showed that the book could bear the most minute scrutiny as an authority for the facts of the Aegean world, and that it was written with such judgement, skill, art and perception of truth as to be a model of historical statement.'[51]

Ramsay continued:

'I set out to look for truth on the borderland where Greece and Asia meet, and found it here [in Acts]. You may press the words of Luke in a degree beyond any other historian's and they stand the keenest scrutiny and the hardest treatment...'[52]

Perhaps no greater comment on the trustworthiness of Luke has ever been made than this. We may therefore wonder why this is not more often acknowledged and why the supposed inaccuracies of the New Testament writers are repeated like a mantra by popular writers today. Wilson mocked many critics of his day with the comment: 'Too often, when one reads some foolish criticism, the words of Shakespeare rise in one's memory that here is "folly doctor-like controlling skill."' Often, little has changed.

Two things particularly impressed Ramsay. In the first place, Luke was a historian not to be compared with other ancient historians and writers. They were sometimes right and accurate, and sometimes wrong

---

51 As above, p.85.
52 As above, p.89.

and careless; Luke was always accurate and careful. Secondly, he was interested to notice that 'Scholars who aimed simply at collecting facts, and had evidently no bias either for or against him [Luke] seemed to regard him as a sufficient authority', whereas those who had already set out to prove that the Bible is a false witness dismissed him as untrustworthy. This is a valuable warning from a scholar like Sir William Ramsay. He never found Luke to be in certain error. There are unsolved issues, but unsolved issues are not errors.

When Ramsay turned his attention to Paul's letters, most of which the critics dismissed as forgeries, he concluded that all thirteen New Testament letters that claimed to have been written by Paul were really his. Despite this, Ramsay did not enter the debate about biblical inerrancy—the term was rarely used in his day—he was not a theologian but simply a brilliant historian and archaeologist. Only a small sample can be offered of his detailed examination of the Gospel of Luke and the Acts of the Apostles. See also Book 1 chapter 3 in this series under 'Authentic history' for more on the accuracy of Luke.

GOVERNMENT OFFICIALS

Ramsay found Luke to be well acquainted with the titles used for the town and city officials in the various provinces of Asia, which differed from town to town. When Paul was in Cyprus a *proconsul* was in charge and, although there had been many changes, Luke used the correct title when referring to Sergius Paulus (Acts 13:7).[53] Philippi was accurately described as a Roman colony whose officials Luke calls *stratagoi* ('magistrates' 16:38). At Thessalonica the reference to the *politarchs* ('city officials' 17:6), is now well attested, especially by an inscription from that town presented to the British Museum in 1877 and known as the 'Polytarch Inscription'.[54] In Ephesus the 'officials of the province' are called the *asiarchs* (19:31), exactly the title of those whom we now know controlled religious affairs. At Malta the *protos* ('chief official' 28:7) was in charge.

---

53 See also Anderson and Edwards, *Evidence for the Bible* (Day One Publications, Leominster, 2014), p. 156.
54 As above, p. 158.

All these titles Wilson found on inscriptions of that time in the various towns. These are facts that would never be known to later generations and therefore constitute clear evidence that Luke was an eyewitness of all that he meticulously recorded.

ICONIUM AND THE CITIES OF LYCAONIA [55]

It was a seemingly insignificant statement in Acts 14:6 that first caused William Ramsay to suspect that Luke was deserving of more honour as a historian than had generally been given to him. The verse describes what happened when Paul and Barnabas were forced to leave the city of Iconium on account of a plot by the Jews: 'They ... fled to the Lycaonian cities of Lystra and Derbe and to the surrounding country.' It had long been believed that the city of Iconium was the chief city of the Roman province of Lycaonia and therefore the statement that Paul and Barnabas fled from Iconium 'to the cities of Lycaonia' showed that the writer had little knowledge of geography at that time.

Ramsay produced a host of detailed evidence to show that Luke was quite right. Whilst Iconium lay in the geographical area of Lycaonia, at the time of Paul's journeys it was a city in the Roman province of Phrygia. In fact the citizens of Iconium were of altogether different stock and did not even speak the Lycaonian language—a fact that obviously impressed itself upon Paul (Acts 14:11). In 1910 Ramsay discovered evidence of a separate Phrygian dialect in Iconium. Not until AD 372 was the province of Lycaonia reformed by the Emperor Valens and Iconium made its capital city. Modern scholars had never gone further back than AD 372 and therefore ignored Luke's evidence, which was correct. From Acts 14:5 to 6 Paul crossed a political and cultural frontier from Phrygia to Lycaonia. This fact is now universally accepted.

Two examples from Ramsay will be sufficient from his wide evidence. In AD 163 the Christian leader Justin, together with several other Christians, was put on trial in Rome. One of these Christians was a slave named Hierax who, when asked who his parents were, replied, 'My earthly

---

55 *The Bearing of Recent Discovery*, pp. 53–78.

parents are dead, and I have been brought here [as a slave] torn away from Iconium of Phrygia.' Pliny, the Roman governor of Bithynia early in the second century AD, referred to Iconium as one of the ancient and famous cities of Phrygia.

Every detail in the story recorded by Luke in Acts 14 was found by Ramsay to be so accurate that he reversed his judgement on Luke as a historian. He was prepared to trust Luke from now on because 'No writer is correct by mere chance, or accurate sporadically. He is accurate by virtue of a certain habit of mind.' Luke had been condemned as unreliable everywhere because of this supposed blunder in Acts 14:6, so when that 'blunder' was shown to be accurate historical reporting, the same reasoning must allow him to be trusted elsewhere. That is exactly what Ramsay found him to be. Both in his Gospel and the record of the infant church in Acts, when Luke writes of cities or slaves, languages or customs, prophets or poets, travel or trials, government officers or religious leaders, merchants or magicians, not only is Luke's variety remarkable, but his accuracy is without equal.

For more on the accuracy of Luke as a historian see Book 1 chapter 3 in this series.

THE CENSUS IN PALESTINE [56]

For many years, Luke 2:1–4 appeared to be an example of the author's historical ignorance; scholars dismissed it, and it was hard to defend because there were so few facts available outside the Bible:

'In those days Caesar Augustus issued a decree that a census should be taken of the entire Roman world. This was the first census that took place while Quirinius was governor of Syria. And everyone went to his own town to register. So Joseph and Mary also went up from the town of Nazareth in Galilee to Judaea, to Bethlehem the town of David...'

The criticisms ran like this:

1. The emperor never issued any decree ordering a census.

---

56 *The Bearing of Recent Discovery*, pp. 238–300.

2. Never, under the Roman emperors, was any regular census ordered.

3. Where a casual census was ordered, only the husband was required to register; the wife did not have to accompany him.

4. On such occasions the husband was not required to return to his place of birth in order to register.

5. Quirinius was not governor of Syria until AD 5–6, that is, nine years after the death of Herod in 4 BC, in whose reign Jesus was born.[57] Both Tertullian, an early Christian leader born around the year AD 155, and Josephus, the Jewish historian born in AD 37, claim that Sentius Saturninus was governor in Syria from 8–6 BC and took the census when Jesus was born.

6. Quirinius called a census in AD 6 and Luke must have mistakenly placed it during the reign of Herod.

7. The story of Joseph and Mary at Bethlehem was therefore entirely false as were all the details surrounding it.

These were the 'certain results of critical scholarship' more than a hundred years ago. We now turn to Sir William Ramsay's answer to these accusations.

1. When Egypt came under the authority of Rome in 30 BC, the Roman emperor left undisturbed the Egyptian system of an annual census. So it is not true to claim that no emperor ever ordered a census. In addition to this, the letters of Pliny, a Roman governor of Bithynia, reveal quite clearly that a regular census was taken in the Roman Empire.[58] So

---

57 The reference to the death of Herod in 4 BC may seem confusing in the light of Matthew 2:19 that Mary and Joseph returned from Egypt to Nazareth 'after Herod died'. When our present dating system was fixed by a monk in the year AD 533, he made a few mistakes in his calculations—including the fact that the Emperor Augustus reigned under his name Octavian for four years before assuming the title 'August'. Christ's birth is probably to be dated in the year 5 BC.

58 In Luke 2:1, Luke may have been referring only to Judaea because the word *oikoumene* can refer to the whole world, the Roman world or even a locality (as in Acts 24:5). In Josephus' *Antiquities* 12:48 it clearly refers to Judaea.

accurate was this system that when, in AD 48, the authorities were suspicious of a man who claimed to be 150 years old, the emperor Claudius ordered a check of past enrolments to test the man's claim; his ages given in previous enrolments corroborated his claim.[59] Therefore, censuses must have been taken regularly.

2. There is definite evidence of enrolments around the years 28 and 8 BC and AD 14, 34, 48, 62 and 76. In other words, it would appear that the emperor ordered an empire-wide census on a regular basis. Ramsay presented clear evidence for this regular census system of the Romans.

3 and 4. A papyrus document [now held in the British Library] of a Roman census in Egypt in the time of the Emperor Titus dated AD 104, orders 'it is essential that all those who are away from their homes be summoned to return to their own hearths.'[60] Ramsay demonstrated that this 'order to return to the home was regularly issued and enforced', and included the whole family.

These first four points are now universally admitted and so, reluctantly, the critics have to acknowledge that Luke was recording historical facts. But what of the problem concerning Quirinius?

5 and 6. There is no question that Quirinius was governor of Syria in AD 6 and that he organized a census during this period of his office. Luke himself knew this and refers to the census in Acts 5:37. It is therefore very unlikely that such an accurate historian would mistakenly place this governorship of AD 6 back in 4 BC. Ramsay needed to show that Quirinius held office in Syria within a year either way of 4 BC.

We know that Quirinius was a consul in Rome in 12 BC but this, Ramsay maintained, was intended to prepare him to take command of a large army to fight the emperor's war in Syria shortly after this date. Ramsay discovered an inscription in Antioch, a leading military stronghold in Syria, that revealed Sulpicius Quirinius was a chief

---

59 Pliny's *Natural History* VII. 48. 159 referenced in *The Bearing of Recent Discovery*, p. 240.
60 See above, *Evidence for the Bible*, p. 117.

magistrate of the city in 8 BC. However, according to the inscription, Quirinius' office was an honorary position and a deputy carried out the duties. Also, according to the inscription, Quirinius appears to have shared the office of chief magistrate with M Servelius. The reason for this arrangement was that Quirinius was fighting the emperor's war against the tribal Hasmonadenses in Syria. This war lasted from 10 to 8 BC and the final resettlement of Syria would possibly require another two years. Clearly then Quirinius could have held the chief post of the Roman legions fighting in Syria during the last years of the reign of King Herod in Palestine.

However, Tertullian, as we have seen, tells us that Sentius Saturninus was governor of Syria at the time of Jesus' birth and it was he who ordered the census. Servelius left office in 6 BC. Josephus gives the date of 8–6 BC for this census. So at least there is good evidence to show that there was a census around the time of Jesus' birth. A full census, requiring people to travel long distances, could take a few years to complete. Ramsay suggests that Quirinius was military governor and Sentius was administrative governor for a short period together. Sentius may have ordered the census and Quirinius, possibly staying on after Sentius had left, actually carried out the command in 6 or 4 BC. We know that Quirinius had moved to Asia as proconsul by 3 BC.

There is still a degree of uncertainty in this whole subject, not because Luke's account has been shown to be wrong, but because we do not have sufficient evidence to show every part of it to be correct. However, all that Ramsay discovered—and there is little more since then—demonstrates that Luke's account has the right to be accepted as trustworthy. Luke's detailed accuracy elsewhere earns him the right to be believed at this point. Professor F F Bruce wisely commented on Luke's historical accuracy: 'If his trustworthiness is vindicated in points where he can be checked, we should not assume that he is less trustworthy where we cannot test his accuracy.'[61]

61 F F Bruce, *The Acts of the Apostles—the Greek text with introduction and commentary* (The Tyndale Press, London 1962), p. 17.

[More recently it has been suggested that Luke 2:2 could be translated: 'This census was before the one made when Quirinius was governor of Syria.' This is acceptable as an alternative translation and if it is correct there is no need to find Quirinius in Syria in 4 BC. However, since Ramsay *has* found evidence of this, the alternative translation is superfluous.]

Many of Sir William Ramsay's arguments are exhaustive and detailed. These few examples illustrate his assessment that the writer of Acts 'has now been found to show excellent knowledge and the minute accuracy which comes from the faithful report of an eyewitness and participator in the action.' The years of patient and careful research, and the thousands of pages that William Ramsay devoted to Luke's Gospel and Acts all show that the customs and language, the synagogues, trials, councils, magicians, in fact everything mentioned, reveal a detailed knowledge that could only be written down by an eye-witness of the events.

CONCLUSION

Although both Wilson and Ramsay were working and writing almost a century ago, they are typical of others who have shown that diligent research has always vindicated the accuracy of biblical history. Unfortunately, many critics today choose simply to ignore the scholarship of Wilson and Ramsay. This fact did not escape Professor F F Bruce, who commented, 'I am repeatedly amazed by modern writers who deal with areas of New Testament scholarship to which Ramsay made contributions of peculiar value, with hardly so much as a hint that such a person ever lived.'[62] Similarly, Professor Kitchen from the University of Liverpool lamented, 'Biblical studies have long been hindered by the persistence of long-outdated philosophical and literary theories (especially of the nineteenth-century stamp).'[63]

In view of the known accuracy of the Bible, where there are still problems unsolved it is reasonable to accept the biblical account and wait

---

62 As above, Preface to second edition 1952, p. viii.
63 Kenneth A Kitchen, *The Bible in its World: The Bible and Archaeology Today* (The Paternoster Press, Exeter. UK 1977).

in the knowledge that eventually an answer will be found. Nowhere has the Bible been found unquestionably false.

Professor Robert Dick Wilson claimed to give his students: 'such an intelligent faith in the Old Testament Scriptures that they will never doubt them as long as they live'. Sir William Mitchell Ramsay maintained that, 'Christianity did not originate in a lie, and we can and ought to demonstrate this, as well as to believe it.'

That is sense as well as faith. They are no fools who agree with men of the intellectual calibre of Wilson and Ramsay.

3. Digging up the evidence

'Archaeology, correctly understood, always confirms the accuracy of the Bible'—Professor Donald J Wiseman (late Professor Emeritus of Assyriology at the University of London).

Ancient civilizations built their towns on top of the rubble, often with the rubble, of the previous occupants. All that the earlier people left behind: their building materials, pottery, jewellery, messages, food remains, household utensils, weapons and even their own bones. These were covered over and therefore preserved for later generations to unearth. Archaeology is the science of reading history from these 'leftovers' of previous civilizations; it is learning who the people were, and when and how they lived. Archaeology has been called 'the study of durable rubbish.'

As generation after generation built on top of the rubbish of their ancestors, or of the enemy they defeated, so the town grew higher and higher. The great mountain of earth that betrays the presence of an old city is called a *tell* a Hebrew word meaning 'ruin mound'. In Arabic it is *tall*. The word *tell* (often spelt *tel*) is found in the Old Testament (2 Kings 19:12 Tel Assar and Ezekiel 3:15 Tel Abib) which indicates that seven hundred years before Jesus Christ, many cities already had a long history. Megiddo, captured by Joshua and fortified by Solomon, is mentioned in Joshua 12:21 and in 1 Kings 9:15–19. The *tell*, now called Tell el Mutesellim, is twenty-one metres high (sixty-eight feet) with the summit covering more than ten acres. It stands isolated on the north side of the Carmel ridge, commanding the pass from the coastal plain to the valley of Esdraelon. The excavation of Megiddo began in 1903 and reveals twenty main occupation levels from 4,000 to 600 BC. Stables for four hundred and fifty horses, perhaps built in the time of King Solomon or King Ahab of Israel, have been discovered.

The story of archaeology

Unfortunately, before archaeology became a true science, grave robbers plundered the gold and silver of many ancient royal tombs and other sites. In the year 530 BC the powerful Persian King Cyrus (Ezra 1:1) died whilst on a campaign to the east. A magnificent tomb was built at Pasargadae for the great ruler. The massive stone-roofed tomb was approached by a platform with seven steps, and above the entrance was the message: 'O man, whoever you are and whenever you come, for I know that you will come—I am Cyrus, who gave the Persians their empire. Do not grudge me this patch of earth that covers my body.' Somebody did begrudge him his resting place, and when Alexander the Great climbed the steps to inspect the tomb in 322 BC, he discovered that the robes, cape, jewellery and scimitar of Cyrus were gone, the stone coffin was shattered and his bones lay all over the floor. The same happened to almost all the tombs of the pharaohs of Egypt. Fortunately, they missed the one belonging to Tutankhamun. There are still many today who are robbing valuable archaeological sites.

The word archaeology comes from the Greek word *archaios* meaning 'ancient'. The Greeks used the word *archaiologia* to refer to a traditional story or legend, and Bishop Hall of Norwich in 1607 employed the word to refer to Bible narratives. It was not until the early nineteenth century that the word described the study of items that were dug out of the ground. An archaeologist became a historian with a bucket and spade. Today its meaning is much broader, and it refers to the study of anything from the past, including old documents. Archaeology is a fascinating science that has added immensely to our understanding of Bible times and events. It is also an ongoing science of discovery and new finds come to light each year.

In recent years, archaeologists tunnelling along the western wall of the temple in Jerusalem discovered five great foundation stones that formed part of the base of the temple of Jesus' day. The largest is around 6 m long (20 ft), 2.1 m high (7 ft) and 3.6 m wide (12 ft). It is estimated to weigh some 570 tons. Such a find certainly makes what Jesus prophesied about the stones of the temple even more dramatic (Matthew 24:1–2). In June 2004 two archaeologists discovered, almost by accident, the original Pool of Siloam in Jerusalem referred to in the story of the healing of the blind man (John 9:1–11); the one that tourists have been accustomed to visit was a much later date. Exciting new finds are still coming to light.

NAPOLEON AND ARCHAEOLOGY

When Napoleon invaded Egypt in 1798, he was interested in the history of his new conquest and he took with him a team of scientists and historians. A year later he had been defeated by the British on land and sea and his army, together with some of the valuable 'treasures' that his scientists had unearthed, were left behind as he sailed away from Egypt. Many of these treasures found their way to the British Museum in London.

Among them was the Rosetta Stone that, once deciphered, assisted Thomas Young and Jean-François Champollion in unlocking the mysteries of Egyptian hieroglyphics. Egyptian archaeological exploration had begun. In spite of their military defeat by the British, French archaeologists remained at the forefront of exploration in Egypt, and it was not until 1883 that the Egypt Exploration Fund was formed in Britain, spearheaded by William Flinders Petrie who opposed those who merely hunted for museum pieces and he bitterly lamented that, 'Our museums are ghostly charnel-houses of murdered evidence.'

Meanwhile, far away to the east, the land of Iraq became a centre of attention also. In 1807, Claudius James Rich was the representative of the British East India Company in Baghdad and, a master of many languages, he toured some of the ruin mounds of ancient Babylonia. He discovered clay tablets with strange writing on them and published his findings; the writing later became known as cuneiform (meaning 'wedge shaped') and the 'code' was finally deciphered three decades later by Sir Henry Rawlinson.

Unfortunately, Rich died at the age of thirty-three before he was able to begin any serious 'digging' but, impressed by his work, the French were the first to fund a proper expedition. Between 1843 and 1845 Paul Emile Botta discovered the city of Khorsabad, the residence of Sargon, king of Assyria. The sensational importance of this find we will see later.

Botta teamed up with a British adventurer, Austen Henry Layard (pronounced Laird), who had become fascinated with the ancient land of Babylon. Between 1849 and 1851, Layard uncovered the fabulous palace of Sennacherib (Sargon's son) at Nineveh. Rooms lined with two miles of stone carvings were discovered, including the famous depiction in stone of Sennacherib's siege and destruction of Lachish in the time of Hezekiah. This was the first archaeological confirmation of an event in the Bible, and is still today the best contemporary evidence of siege warfare available anywhere so far discovered. We will look at this in more detail later.

In 1872, George Smith working from the British Museum, discovered ancient Babylonian stories of creation and a flood. By the middle of the nineteenth century interest had spread to the land of the New Testament, The first major archaeological exploration of Palestine was conducted by two Americans, Edward Robinson and Eli Smith; they assumed that the Bible was true and allowed it to comment on their discoveries. French, English, and German archaeologists were soon busy adding to our knowledge of the lands of the Bible, and the Palestine Exploration Fund was set up in 1865; the American Palestine Exploration Society was formed in 1870, and in the same year the British Society of Biblical Archaeology. Rules were eventually laid down for digging, recording, protecting and even exporting the items found. Archaeology had become the respected, scholarly and intensely skilful science that it is today.

In broad outline, archaeology in the lands associated with the Bible, has moved through a number of phases: from gathering items for museums, to uncovering material that would endorse the reliability of the Bible, to archaeological research for its own sake irrespective of conclusions, and finally—in the minds of some today—to gathering information that would disprove the Bible.

Today, carefully managed museums across the world display thousands of Bible-related items. Among them: The Bible Lands Museum in Jerusalem, The Museum of Egyptian Antiquities in Cairo, The Louvre in Paris, The Metropolitan Museum in New York, The University of

Chicago Oriental Institute, The Pergamon Museum in Berlin, and The British Museum in London.[64]

Archaeology illustrates
the culture and customs of Bible times

Archaeology often helps us to appreciate a fuller meaning of the text. This is immensely valuable in assisting those who study the Bible to gain a clearer understanding of what lies behind the biblical record. One archaeologist expressed this well when he claimed that the purpose of biblical archaeology is, 'To read the Bible in the setting of its time, its people, its land, to reconstruct its history and to study its literature and religion comparatively.'[65] Archaeology covers every period of Bible history and possibly its greatest value is not to 'prove the Bible true', but to throw light onto the details of everyday life in Bible times; it is an aid to our understanding of the customs and culture, the religion and ideas of the nations that significantly affected the Jews, and of Israel itself.[66]

CIVILIZATION IN THE TIME OF ABRAHAM[67]

'Terah took his son Abram … and his daughter-in-law Sarai … and together they set out from Ur of the Chaldeans to go to Canaan. But when they came to Haran, they settled there' (Genesis 11:31). Ur is one hundred and twenty miles north of Basra in Iraq. In 1926 Sir Leonard Woolley excavated the site of Ur, the city of Abraham's birth, including many royal tombs; his discoveries revealed the advanced state of civilization at Ur centuries before Abraham. The patriarch could have lived in a two-storey brick house with a lobby, courtyard, kitchen and toilet, bedrooms and reception rooms;

---

64 For an item by item tour of the Bible-related exhibits in the British Museum see Edwards and Anderson, *Through the British Museum with the Bible* (Day One Publications, Leominster UK). It provides clear directions, together with pictures and a description of all the main exhibits. It can be purchased in the Museum or ordered on-line from Day One.

65 G E Wright 'Biblical Archaeology Today' (1966) in *New Directions in Biblical Archaeology* ed. Freedman and Greenfield. (Doubleday, New York 1969), p.151.

66 Many of the following examples are described and illustrated in Clive Anderson and Brian Edwards, *Evidence for the Bible* (Day One Publications, Leominster UK 2014).

67 *Evidence for the Bible*, pp.4,6.

Sarah would have been accustomed to seeing royalty wear beautifully intricate head-dresses and jewellery, and may have worn some herself.

Tablets of clay and a small square-ended spatula were the paper and pencil of Abraham's day; baked hard in the sun, the completed document would last almost indefinitely. Thousands of these official records in cuneiform writing reveal a bustling city of merchants and businessmen trading into Syria and down to the Persian Gulf. They record purchases, marriages, and all the events of the life of a busy city, including complaints for the delivery of the wrong or inferior merchandise! There were even tablets used by teachers to help children learn to read and write, which were of immense help in deciphering cuneiform. Details of their ancient religion are also represented. The priests were busy with their elaborate duties at the gigantic temple (Ziggurat) of the moon god Sin.

Abraham, long thought by some to be a primitive nomadic tribesman, came from a city of culture and comforts. Cities of the same date, excavated in the same region, reveal that these people had a correct understanding of algebra, mathematics (including quantum maths), and geometry— including the theorem of Pythagoras, nearly fifteen hundred years before the Greek philosopher was born.

The great city of Ebla, though not mentioned in the Bible, was situated not far from Haran, the town from which Abraham was called by God into the desert. The tell of Ebla—Tell Mardikh in north west Syria—was positively identified in 1975 and since then valuable information has come from the clay tablets in the archive room of the royal palace. This city was flourishing in the time of Abraham, with a population at one period of more than a quarter of a million.

Similarly, the ancient city of Mari, capital of the Amorites, provided over 20,000 texts revealing the active life of a palace with nearly six hundred rooms. Daniel Fleming, an expert in the Mari texts, concludes that these demonstrate that the narratives of the patriarchs accurately reflect the culture of that time.[68] Personal names similar to Noah, Abram, Laban,

---

68 *The Future of Biblical Archaeology—Reassessing Methodologies and Assumptions*, ed. James K Hoffmeier and Alan Millard (Eerdmans Publishing Co., Grand Rapids and Cambridge 2004), pp. 203–205.

Jacob, Gad, Dan, Levi, and Ishmael appear in the texts and show that such names were common at this period. A city named Nahur (Nahor of Genesis 11:22–25?) is mentioned, as well as the city of Haran (Genesis 11:31 to12:4). Hazor is referred to often, and there is a reference to Laish (Dan) and an Arioch (Genesis 14:1). The Mari texts claim that at this time 'there is no king strongest by himself', which is exactly reflected in the book of Genesis.

For many years, critics claimed that Moses could not have written the first five books of the Bible because writing had not been invented around 1500 BC. Royal libraries and archives, pre-dating Abraham (2000 BC) reveal huge amounts of written material; Leonard Woolley discovered that almost a quarter of all the houses in Abraham's home town of Ur contained writing material.

Archaeology has not yet uncovered any evidence that refers directly to the patriarchs—Abraham, Isaac and Jacob—although their names, as we have seen from Mari, are familiar to the period. However, whilst the patriarchs are crucial figures in the history of Judaism and Christianity, they became little more than wandering nomads in their time. They led no great armies, ruled over no empire, and their religion precluded them leaving monuments and inscriptions to their own credit.

Many of the details of their stories agree with what we learn from archaeology. For example, the twenty silver shekels that the Midianites paid for Joseph (Genesis 37:28) is precisely what we know to be the price of a slaves in that region at that time. Professor James Hoffmeier points out that since the price of slaves rose steeply over the next thousand years to ninety shekels, if the stories had been written long after the event—as some critics claim—no author could possibly have known the price of slaves at the time of Joseph.[69]

THE LAW OF MOSES AND POEMS OF BABYLON[70]

Frequently, assumptions are made that biblical accounts are 'borrowed' from ancient records. However, the verse that introduces the laws given to

---

69 James K Hoffmeier, *Israel in Egypt* (Oxford University Press, Oxford/New York 1996), pp. 83–84.
70 *Evidence for the Bible*, pp. 24, 25.

Moses on Mount Sinai begins, 'And God spoke all these words' (Exodus 20:1). Hammurabi lived in Babylon possibly two hundred years before Moses was born in Egypt. Some of the laws of his kingdom were carefully chiselled onto a stone pillar two and a quarter metres high, and now in the Musée de Louvre in Paris. These laws contain some similarities to the laws of Moses found in Exodus 21–23. However, there are many significant differences. See Book 1 chapter 6 in this series under 'A unique religion—ancient law codes' for the contrast with the Hammurabi code. The laws given by Moses clearly have a higher view of the value of life. There is no need to suppose, as some critics do, that Moses 'borrowed' ideas from the Hammurabi Code.

Moses' laws came from God himself, and the similarities are explained by the fact that there were common concerns in the ancient world. The laws given by Moses put into writing principles that God had given his people over a long period of time, but these were complete by the death of Moses (Joshua 1:7–8). Indeed the ancient world was intended to benefit from the presence of the patriarchs and Moses and the standards they set (see Deuteronomy 4–8).

No one knows exactly who Job was or when and where his moving account of suffering was written, but it is not alone in 'wisdom literature' in the ancient world. One of the best known poems from Babylon is 'The poem of the righteous sufferer', and its author has been referred to as 'the Babylonian Job'. However, one expert on the Babylonians comments that this title is unmerited because: 'The biblical work, by its spiritual insight and beauty of imagery soars so high above the Babylonian that the two can scarcely be compared.'[71] Unlike the account of Job, it makes no attempt to explore the mysteries of suffering and offers nothing that could be of value today. But at least it reflects the popularity of this kind of 'wisdom literature' two millennia before Christ.

---

71 H W F Saggs, *The Babylonians—A survey of the ancient civilisations of the Tigris-Euphrates Valley* (1988), The London Folio Society, 1999, p. 359.

THE FLOOD IN ANCIENT LEGENDS[72]

Whilst there are ancient stories of creation—the best known is the so called *Atrahasis epic*—they bear little or no resemblance to the biblical story. However, with the flood it is different. In 1872, George Smith, an assistant working at the British Museum, deciphered some clay tablets that were part of the library in Nineveh, the city of Ashurbanipal who was the last king of Assyria (668–627 BC). Ashurbanipal, the grandson of Sennacherib, was the 'Osnapper' of Ezra 4:10 (the word used in the original Aramaic of this verse), and the 'king of Assyria' referred to in 2 Chronicles 33:11. George Smith found he was reading a seventh-century BC copy of an ancient Babylonian story of a great flood. There is archaeological evidence that this story was widespread across the ancient Orient (there are even fragments of it from Palestine and Turkey) back to the time of Abraham.

The *Gilgamesh epic* is a poem of two hundred lines, about Gilgamesh who searches for Utanapishtim in order to enquire about immortality. Utanapishtim recounts the story of his own search, which involved the great flood. In the epic, Utanapishtim is ordered by his god, the benevolent Ea, to build an ark in order to escape the flood with which the council of gods planned to destroy the earth. Although there are many differences, it is impossible to read the story without recognising close similarities with the biblical account of Noah: the offending mortals on earth, the one to be rescued, the building of an ark to house Utanapishtim's family and the animals, the awesome and destructive flood, the release of birds from the boat and finally the offering of a sacrifice to the gods; Ea even addresses the gods and asserts that the punishment was too severe and nothing like this must happen again. Incidentally, Gilgamesh did not obtain his desired immortality.

Although there are many significant differences—not least a cluster of evil quarrelling gods who themselves become terrified by the flood—there can be little doubt that the Babylonian story reflects the persistent legends of a global flood, which is recorded in Genesis 6. From the list of Sumerian kings comes a similar story from Mesopotamia, somewhere between the time of

---

72 *Evidence for the Bible*, pp. 2, 3.

Joseph and Moses. This time the gods are concerned that man is becoming too numerous and noisy, and they plan a flood to reduce the numbers. In this *Atrakhasis epic* it is Atrakhasis whom the god Enlil orders to build a boat.

Not surprisingly, the story of a great flood is one of the most widely held stories in the world. The ancient literature of more than thirty nations contain flood stories, including Persia, Siberia, Africa, Greece, China, the Aborigines of Australia, the Maoris of New Zealand, the Eskimos of Alaska and the Red Indians of North America. The most natural explanation for these stories passed on as legend in many cultures across the world, is the reality of the account related in Genesis 6.

ODDS AND ENDS

Sling stones were discovered at the gate of the ruin mound of Lachish from the battle that took place in 701 BC and is referred to in 2 Chronicles 32:9. They reveal that the stones, with a diameter of 44 mm, were a little larger than a billiard ball. The wall panels from Nineveh depicting the Assyrian 'slingers' show the vital significant of this as the artillery of the ancient world. All of which throws light on the combat between David and Goliath and the size of the 'five smooth stones' the shepherd boy would have gathered (1 Samuel 17:40).[73]

The reference in 1 Samuel 17:57 that David came before Saul 'still holding the Philistine's head', and the statement in 2 Kings 10:7 that the heads of Saul's seventy sons were presented to Jehu in a basket, are not gruesomely irrelevant details. Wall panels of ancient warfare show soldiers being awarded for their skill in battle with enemy heads at their feet. This was the only certain way of identifying the slain warrior.

A wall panel of the Assyrian king Tiglath-Pileser III with his feet firmly on the neck of a grovelling enemy is reflected in Joshua's command to his captains after the capture of five kings: '"Come here and put your feet on the necks of these kings." So they came forward and placed their feet on their necks.' (Joshua 10:24). It was a customary way of demonstrating the total defeat and submission of the enemy.

---

73 *Evidence for the Bible*, p. 71.

The prophet warned Israel: 'you will be taken away with hooks. The last of you with fish-hooks' (Amos 4:2), and Chronicles records that the Assyrian army 'took Manasseh prisoner, put a hook in his nose, bound him with bronze shackles and took him to Babylon' (2 Chronicles 33:11). This is illustrated by a stela of Esarhaddon of Assyria showing the king holding a defeated enemy at the end of a hook in his lips and nose.[74]

Wall reliefs at Karnak in Egypt that illustrate Egyptian women giving birth by sitting on a stool, allowing the baby to drop, provides the background to the 'delivery stool' referred to in Exodus 1:16.

The biblical account of Esther, a queen in Persia to the great king Xerxes, is rightly concerned with the threat to destroy all Jews within the empire and gives only a little hint of the fabulous wealth of the Persians. Archaeology can add colour to Esther's banquet (Esther 5:4). Here is a description of a later Persian king's banquet: 'The courtyard was decorated with blue and white cotton curtains, tied by cords of fine purple linen to silver rings on marble columns. Couches made of gold and silver had been placed in the courtyard, which was paved with white marble, red feldspar, shining mother-of-pearl, and blue turquoise.' Alexander the Great is alleged to have discovered over 120 tons of gold in the palace at Susa. The great Audience Hall (Esther 5:1) has also been uncovered and Esther approached the Great King on his throne in a hall glittering with carvings, colourful painting, tapestries and carpets.[75]

In the time of Jesus, an inscription on a large limestone block warned non-Jews, on pain of death, not to pass beyond the 'court of the Gentiles' into the precincts of Herod's temple reserved only for Jews. Discovered in 1871, this warning which was originally vividly painted in red, was clearly in the mind of Paul when he wrote to the Ephesian Christians: 'He [Jesus] himself is our peace, who has made the two one and has destroyed the barrier, the dividing wall of hostility' (Ephesians 2:14).[76]

---

74 *Evidence for the Bible*, p. 77.
75 A vivid and detailed description is given in Alan Millard, *Treasures from Bible Times* (Lion Publishing plc, Tring, UK. 1985), pp. 141–145.
76 *Evidence for the Bible*, p. 147.

The number of terracotta masks used by actors that have been found are graphic illustrations of the Greek word *hupocrites*[77] used frequently by Jesus to condemn the Pharisees of his day (Matthew 23:13–29). This was the word used of the actor's mask and metaphorically became a description of someone who was 'two-faced'.[78]

In the same context, Jesus referred to the teachers of the law and the Pharisees who sat 'in Moses' seat' (Matthew 23:2). This was a literal seat reserved in the synagogues for the most important teachers of the Law of Moses. One such seat was discovered at Chorazin. Jesus condemned the teachers for sitting in 'Moses seat' yet not obeying the Law themselves.[79]

In 2 Timothy 4:13 Paul requested young Timothy to bring with him several personal items belonging to the apostle; this included 'my scrolls, especially the parchments'. That last word translated the Latin word *membranae*. It referred to thin strips of wood or leather held together by rings; it was a 'ring-binder', or first century notebook. The Greeks had no name for it, so they borrowed the Latin word. A few of these have been discovered and show clearly the sort of notebook that Paul was using.

Much has been discovered in the ruins of the ancient city of Laodicea, including the furred water pipes that brought the lukewarm water from the hills, that illustrate the references to the city in Revelation 3.

Archaeology authenticates the accuracy of biblical history

One of most brilliant professional scholars and archaeologist of the twentieth century, Professor Donald J Wiseman claimed, 'Archaeology, correctly understood, always confirms the accuracy of the Bible.'[80] We have seen in the previous chapter the same conclusion from two outstanding scholars from earlier in that century. Whilst it is true that archaeology is

---

77 *Evidence for the Bible*, p. 145.
78 *Evidence for the Bible*, p. 126.
79 *Evidence for the Bible*, p. 129.
80 In a personal conversation with the author. Professor Donald Wiseman, who died in 2010, was Professor Emeritus of Assyriology in the University of London, formerly Assistant Keeper in the Egyptian and Western Asiatic Antiquities at the British Museum, and President of the British School of Archaeology in Iraq.

valuable in throwing light on Bible times, it can also support the claim that the Bible is reliable in all its history. There are many examples of people or events that critics assumed had no real history because the only record was in the Bible. All of these are accepted today.[81]

WHO WERE THE HITTITES?[82]

At one time the only known references to the Hittites were their frequent mention in the Bible (Genesis 10:15; 15:20; 23:3 etc). This led some scholars to question their existence, even though from the biblical record they were clearly a powerful, feared and important people. In 1906 their ancient capital of Hattusas, now Boğhazköy in Turkey, was uncovered and they are known to have been an enlightened, educated people and powerful. The Hittite empire was founded around 1700 BC, and from 1400 the Hittites became one of the great powers, in diplomatic and trade contact with other kings. Pharaoh Ramesses II left on record his battle against them at Kadesh in 1274. By 1200 BC Hittite power was broken and their empire declined.

DAVID A LEGENDARY HERO?[83]

Because there was no reference to David outside the Bible, some scholars assumed that the biblical David was a legendary hero invented by scribes somewhere after the sixth century BC to bolster the morale of the Jews in the Babylonian/Persian exile.

An inscription, found at Tell Dan in Northern Israel in 1993, comes from the time of Hazael of Syria just before 800 BC. This 'Tel Dan inscription' refers to 'the king of Israel … and the king of *Bayt-Dawid*'. It is almost universally accepted that the final phrase can only be translated 'House (dynasty) of David'. It is a clear reference to the existence of King David. Therefore, 250 years before the stories of David were supposed to have been invented, he was recognised as the founder of the kingdom of Judah.

---

81 For details and source references for all the following examples see Anderson and Edwards, *Evidence for the Bible* (Day One Publications. Leominster UK, 2014).

82 *Evidence for the Bible*, p. 33.

83 *Evidence for the Bible*, pp. 36–37.

The 'Mesha Stela'—or 'Moabite Stone' is another early evidence of David. Most scholars are convinced that David is also mentioned in this inscription. Dated around 840 BC it places the reference only 120 years after David's death.

SARGON—THE KING WHO NEVER LIVED?[84]

The only known reference to Sargon was found in Isaiah 20:1, and therefore critics assumed that such a king never existed.

In 1843, Paul-Emil Botta uncovered the great city of Dur-Sharrukin— 'Sargon's Fortress'—on the banks of the River Tigris, 12 km (8.5 mi) to the northeast of Nineveh. Sharrukin (Sargon) is now one of the best-known Assyrian kings and was one of the most powerful rulers in the ancient world. His library and administrative offices revealed thousands of clay documents. His palace, containing 240 rooms, was guarded by huge human-headed winged bulls each weighing around ten tons and standing 4.8 m (15 ft) high. The walls were lined with great slabs of stone carved with pictures and cuneiform writing. We now have an incredible store of knowledge of this man, including the fact that one of his daughters was both a priestess and a poetess.

This is the Assyrian king who completed the destruction of Samaria in 722 BC, and his own record claims, 'In the first year of my reign I besieged and conquered the town of Samaria, led away as prisoners 27,290 inhabitants of it … and settled therein people from countries which I myself had conquered.'[85] He also carried off 'the gods in whom they trusted'—evidence of how far Israel had strayed from the worship of Yahweh alone.

In fact, it was Sargon's predecessor Shalmaneser V, referred to in 2 Kings 17:3–4 and 2 Kings 18:9, who began the siege; however, he died after two years, and Sargon completed the work. Interestingly in 2 Kings 17:6 and 18:10, when the fall of Samaria is recorded after the three-year

---

84 *Evidence for the Bible*, pp. 60–61.
85 *Ancient Near Eastern Texts*, ed. James B Pritchard(Princeton University Press, Princeton 1950), p. 284.

siege, the name of Shalmaneser is not repeated because it was Sargon who finally broke the Israelite capital.

'LIKE A BIRD IN A CAGE' [86]

In 701 BC, twenty years after the defeat of Samaria by Sargon, his son Sennacherib sent a massive army against Jerusalem when Hezekiah rebelled against him. The account is told in detail in the Bible (2 Kings 18; 2 Chronicles 32; Isaiah 36–37). Sennacherib also left his own record on the 'Taylor Prism' discovered in 1830 by Colonel R Taylor, the British representative in Baghdad. Sennacherib recorded details of his campaign against the Hebrew king including the fact that 'The terrifying splendour of my majesty overcame Hezekiah. The warriors and select troops [Arabs and mercenaries?] he had brought in to strengthen his royal city Jerusalem did not fight.' He acknowledged that although he was unable to take Jerusalem itself, he destroyed the surrounding country:

'As for Hezekiah, the Jew, he did not submit to my yoke, I laid siege to forty-six of his strong cities, walled forts and to the countless small villages in their vicinity, and conquered [them] by means of well-stamped [earth] ramps, and battering-rams brought [thus] near to the walls combined with the attack by foot soldiers, using mines, breeches as well as sapper work. I drove out of them 200,150 people, young and old, male and female, horses, mules, donkeys, camels, big and small cattle beyond counting, and considered them booty. Himself I made a prisoner in Jerusalem, his royal residence, like a bird in a cage.'

When Sennacherib returned to Nineveh, his victory room displayed in elaborate detail the siege and capture of Lachish instead of Jerusalem. This was discovered by Austen Henry Layard in 1849.

This was precisely as the prophet Isaiah records of the same events:

'In the fourteenth year of King Hezekiah's reign, Sennacherib king of Assyria attacked all the fortified cities of Judah and captured them. Then the king of Assyria sent his field commander to King Hezekiah at Jerusalem' (Isaiah 36:1–2).

---

86 *Evidence for the Bible*, p. 75 and *Ancient Near Eastern Texts*, p. 288.

What Sennacherib does not tell us—nor would we expect him to—is that shortly afterwards he lost the bulk of his army by an unseen hand (Isaiah 37:36–37). The biblical account and the Assyrian account of the invasion converge even in details. According to Isaiah 37:38 and 2 Kings 19:37 Sennacherib met a violent death in his palace at Nineveh. Sennacherib's younger son and successor, Esarhaddon, agrees: 'My brothers forsook the gods and turned to their deeds of violence, plotting evil … To gain the kingship they slew Sennacherib their father.'

See in this series Book 1 chapter 2 for more on Isaiah and Sennacherib.

NINEVEH—THE CITY THAT NEVER EXISTED?[87]

In 648 BC Babylon had been burned by the Assyrians after a three year siege, and in 612 Nabopolassar of Babylon captured the Assyrian capital, Nineveh, and wreaked a terrible revenge from which the city never recovered.

The biblical prophet Nahum vividly warned the Assyrians that their powerful empire would end catastrophically and their great capital would be devastated by fire and water (Nahum 3:1–3, 15). Zephaniah similarly had warned the end for the great city: 'leaving Nineveh utterly desolate, as dry as the desert' (Zephaniah 2:13). Nineveh's great palace walls could not be destroyed, even by the fiercest conflagration, and gradually the site covered over so that it seemed that Nineveh had never existed except for the record in the Bible. By the nineteenth century some questioned whether such a great city had ever existed.

In 1847, Austen Henry Layard discovered the palace and its miles of wall reliefs. The fire-blackened walls recovered from the palace at Nineveh revealed just how accurate Nahum's prophecy was. The city that some thought had never existed, had been discovered two and a half thousand years later.

See in this series Book 1 chapter 2 for more on Nineveh and the biblical prophets.

---

87 *Evidence for the Bible*, p. 79.

BELSHAZZAR WHO?[88]

The book of Daniel records how 'King Belshazzar gave a great banquet for a thousand of his nobles … That very night Belshazzar, king of the Babylonians, was slain' (Daniel 5:1,30). At one time critics held that Daniel was clearly in error because no king by the name of Belshazzar had ever been found in any ancient document apart from Daniel 5:22; 7:1; 8:1. The king at the time to which Daniel refers is known to be Nabonidus.

In 1854, J E Taylor, the British Consul at Basra, discovered a small clay cylinder in Ur of the Chaldees (northern Iraq). It proved to be one of four 'time capsules' placed at the corner of a repaired temple to the moon god, and on it was an inscription by Nabonidus, King of Babylon. The inscription was a prayer for the good health and long life of the king, and for 'Bel-sar-usur, my firstborn son, the offspring of my heart.' Today, no one questions the existence of Belshazzar.

The mystery is not quite solved with the discovery of the 'Nabonidus Cylinder'. Among later inscriptions discovered, Belshazzar was always referred to as the 'crown prince'. So, was the king's son ever king himself as Daniel claims? And why was Daniel offered by Belshazzar the post of '*third* highest ruler in the kingdom' (Daniel 5:7,16)?

In 1876 Sir Henry Rawlinson discovered jars filled with over two thousand cuneiform clay tablets, and among them was an account by Cyrus, King of Persia, of his invasion of Babylon, in which he claimed to have taken Nabonidus prisoner but added that on a certain night 'the king died'. Records show that Nabonidus lived as Cyrus' prisoner for many years, therefore the king who died must have been his son Belshazzar, acting as king and of whom the Bible claims, 'That very night Belshazzar, king of the Babylonians, was slain' (Daniel 5:30).

It is now understood that Nabonidus had settled his son as regent of Babylonia when he himself led his army to the north west of Arabia at Teima, which he made his base for the next ten years. From here he pushed more than two hundred and fifty miles deeper into Arabia. For all practical purposes Belshazzar was king in Babylon at the time of the Persian capture

---

88 *Evidence for the Bible*, pp. 92–93.

of the city in 539 BC. With his father still officially on the throne, he could only make Daniel 'third ruler in the kingdom'.

THE CYRUS CYLINDER—GO HOME[89]

2 Chronicles 36:23 (compare Ezra 1:2 and 6:3–5)) reads, 'This is what Cyrus king of Persia says: "The LORD, the God of heaven, has given me all the kingdoms of the earth and he has appointed me to build a temple for him at Jerusalem in Judah. Anyone of his people among you—may his God be with him, and let him go up..."' This was the Cyrus whose tomb in Pasargadae Alexander the Great found to be broken and robbed.

For years, it was assumed that no pagan king would have referred to the Jewish God, or the gods of any of his subject people, in the terms described here; even less would he have given permission for a defeated people to rebuild their temples.

A small clay cylinder, discovered in the ruins of ancient Babylon in 1879, marked the triumph of Cyrus over Babylon in 539 BC and described his capture of Nabonidus (see above). Part of the cylinder reads: 'I am Cyrus, king of all, the great king, the mighty king, king of Babylon, king of Sumer and Akkad, king of the four corners of the earth...' The king then went on to boast of his generous spirit in returning many of the gods captured by Nebuchadnezzar of Babylon to their original temples and the fact that he arranged for the restoration of many temples in Babylonia, Assyria and Iran, and for the return of their people to their homeland.

Although Judah and Jerusalem are not mentioned on the cylinder (one side is almost totally destroyed and who knows whether they were mentioned there?), it demonstrates that such an action was widespread under Cyrus. From other evidence, we know that it was not an uncommon practice in the world of the ancient Orient for victorious kings to begin their rule with magnanimous gestures and reforms.

It is now agreed that 'Cyrus was in fact the first ruler in history who did not simply deport people from the native lands, but rather returned them

---

89 *Evidence for the Bible*, p. 97.

to their homelands with their treasures and sacred temple vessels.'[90] Once more the biblical record was not merely correct, but exact.

The Cyrus Cylinder is considered to be so significant as a 'charter of human rights' that a replica is in the United Nations Headquarters in New York and it has been translated into all the official languages of the UN. Although in the British Museum, it is a national icon of Iran.

See also in this series Book 1 chapter 2 under 'Isaiah and Cyrus of Persia'.

'A CENSUS OF THE ENTIRE ROMAN WORLD'[91]

'This was the first census while Quirinius was governor of Syria ... everyone went to his own town to register' (Luke 2:2). In chapter 2 we considered the response of William Mitchell Ramsay to those who doubted this census. Sufficient here to refer to the papyrus document, discovered in Egypt in 1905, from the year AD 104 when the Roman Prefect of Egypt, Gaius Vibius Maximus ordered all those in his area who were away from 'home', *nomes*—the word refers to an administrative district, to return to their 'hearth', *ephestia*—meaning a place of origin. That is what the census of Caesar Augustus demanded and why Joseph and Mary had to return to Bethlehem.

Many individuals known to history from archaeology are introduced to us in the Bible, including Pilate Governor of Judaea based at his headquarters in Caesarea, Sergius Paulus the Roman governor of Cyprus in AD 47 when Paul and Barnabas landed there (Acts 13:7), Erastus a city official in Corinth in AD 57 (Romans 16:23), Gallio the proconsul of Achaia (Acts 18:12).

All seven men mentioned by Luke when John the Baptist began his ministry are known to history: 'In the fifteenth year of the reign of Tiberius Caesar—when Pontius Pilate was governor of Judaea, Herod tetrarch of Galilee, his brother Philip tetrarch of Iturea and Traconitis, and Lysanias tetrarch of Abilene—during the high priesthood of Annas and Caiaphas, the word of God came to John son of Zechariah in the desert.' (Luke 3:1–2).

---

90 *The Cyrus Cylinder*, Ed. Irving Finkel (I B Taurus, London 2013), p.118.
91 *Evidence for the Bible*, p.117.

The limitation of biblical archaeology

Archaeologist are not infallible.[92] They may misinterpret the evidence or even allow their own prejudice to cloud their conclusion. The story of the archaeology of one significant episode in Israel's history may illustrate this. First claims for a discovery may not be the final claim. Jericho is a warning to the unwary.

THE LOST CITY OF JERICHO [93]

The uncovering of ancient Jericho has become almost a test case in the various swings of archaeological theory. A contemporary view that there were no large cities in Canaan at the time of Joshua obviously has consequences for the biblical account.

The destruction of Jericho is described in Joshua 6. Forty years earlier the strength of the large and well defended cities of Canaan had overawed the Israelites (Numbers 13:27–29; Deuteronomy 1:28). Jericho was plundered by Joshua more than fourteen hundred years before Jesus was born, and again by archaeologists more recently. Scholars have always been interested in the conquest of Canaan by Joshua, and various dates for it have been suggested. Whether the traditional date of 1406 BC for its destruction, or later dates of 1290 or 1230 BC were accepted, a significant problem was that most archaeologists concluded there was no great city on the Jericho site at any of those dates.

- During the 1930s, Professor John Garstang, from the University of Liverpool in England, explored the old city of Jericho and discovered huge walls that had obviously been broken down, and a city that had been plundered and set on fire. By the pottery and other items, Garstang dated the destruction of this city at around 1407 BC. That fitted well the time of Joshua's conquest.

- However, in 1958 Dame Kathleen Kenyon, completed her own research into Jericho and announced that Garstang's dating was wrong. The

---

92 See *Evidence for the Bible*, pp. 211–219 for twelve 'Fallacies of archaeology'.
93 *Evidence for the Bible*, p. 27.

city he had discovered was not the Jericho that Joshua destroyed, but a city on the same site which was destroyed about 1,000 years before Joshua crossed the river Jordan. In fact, Kathleen Kenyon claimed, there was no large city on the site in the time of Joshua. Her conclusions were widely accepted, and even the InterVarsity Press *Illustrated Bible Dictionary* suggested: 'It is possible that in Joshua's day [they accept a 13th century date] there was a small town on the east part of the mound.' Another evangelical writer claimed that: 'There is enough [evidence] to show there were some people about at Jericho somewhere near the time of Joshua's attack.' This was hardly the description of a city 'with walls up to the sky' that so terrified the Israelite spies.

• In 1978 John J Bimson, from Sheffield University, published his own academic research and argued for a fifteenth century date for the Exodus and cast serious doubt upon Kenyon's conclusions.[94] If Bimson is right, then the discussion has come back again to the support of biblical accuracy. On the other hand, many archaeologists are still convinced of a thirteenth century date for the Exodus. It seems that the jury is still out at Jericho.

Demanding evidence for each biblical account is not how historians treat every ancient document. Archaeologists agree with the maxim that: 'The absence of evidence is not evidence of absence'—but many make the Bible an exception and demand evidence for everything. On the contrary, the Bible, having proved itself accurate time and again after rigorous examination, has the right to be accepted as fact until evidence to the contrary is produced.

If we examine the biblical text of the Jericho account, it may not be so difficult to understand why so little remains of the ancient city for archaeologists to discover.

• In the first place, the record in Joshua claims to be an eyewitness account. According to Joshua 6:25 Rahab and her family were still living at the time of the record being written. Secondly, the whole story in Joshua and

---

94 J J Bimson, *Redating the Exodus and Conquest* (Sheffield Press, 1978).

the faithless report forty years earlier of the spies, who spoke about those great cities with walls up to the skies, hardly describe 'a small town on the east part of the mound.' There must have been some reason why the Israelites refused to enter Canaan in the time of Moses.

• Assuming her dating is right, why could Kathleen Kenyon find little trace of this great city? Partly because the Israelites plundered the city of all its silver, gold, bronze and iron (Joshua 6:19) and 'devoted all in the city to destruction' (v. 21 ESV); it is these very items that the archaeologist looks for as traces of civilization. In addition, the 'wall collapsed' so completely, that the Israelite soldiers had no need to rush at gaps but 'every man charged straight in' (v. 20). If the wall that God destroyed for Joshua had been built upon the ruins of the one Garstang found, the destruction was so complete that only those original foundations remained; hence his dating was earlier than Kenyon's.

• There is another and significant reason why Kenyon would be unable to find the remains of Joshua's city. Joshua placed a curse upon anyone who rebuilt it (Joshua 6:26), and the fear of this meant that the ruins of Jericho were left open to the wind and rain for many centuries until Hiel, in the time of Ahab, defied the curse and paid the price for doing so (1 Kings 16:34). Those five centuries of exposure to the elements would have destroyed much of the remains of the city defeated by Joshua. We are therefore not surprised that archaeologists can find little evidence of the site being occupied during these five hundred years and even less evidence of the city Joshua destroyed. For the durable rubbish to be preserved it would be essential that successive towns were built on top of it. This did not happen at Jericho.

These are biblical records that an archaeologist must take into account. No archaeologist can say, 'There certainly was no city with huge walls in the fifteenth century BC at Jericho.' The most he or she can say is, 'So far we have found no evidence of a city with huge walls in the fifteenth century BC at Jericho.' The Bible itself may give the archaeologist a clue as to why this is. Ultimately, it is unwise for a belief in the accuracy of Scripture to depend upon archaeological conclusions.

ARCHAEOLOGICAL PREJUDICE

The earlier comment that some archaeologists demand of the biblical records evidence that they do not insist on from other ancient documents is illustrated by Professor Kenneth Kitchen who criticised those who dismiss the report in 1 Kings 9:16 that Solomon married an Egyptian princess on the sole evidence of the Egyptian Pharaoh Amenophis III (c. 1380 BC) who claimed 'From of old no [Egyptian] king's daughter has been given to anyone.'[95] Kitchen accused these 'Old Testament scholars' of 'arrogance and ignorance' and offered a number of conclusive reasons why their prejudiced conclusion is in error, including:

- Amenophis was writing four hundred years before Solomon, and customs could change.

- The granddaughter of that very same Amenophis III actually offered herself to a Hittite prince.

- Just before the reign of Solomon, Psusennes II (960–945 BC) gave his daughter to a Libyan noble.

Why, we may ask, was not the biblical record accepted as evidence that the Egyptian kings in the time of Solomon *did* in fact marry their daughters to foreign rulers, and that Amenophis III was therefore, referring to an older custom of the Egyptians—or simply 'dishing out xenophobic propaganda'? We may legitimately be suspicious of their scholarship when they *assume* an error in such a proven reliable document as the Hebrew Scriptures.

HEBRON, THE CITY OF DAVID

Second only to Jerusalem, few cities can be more important in the Hebrew Scriptures than Hebron. Its history in the Bible goes back to Genesis (13:18) until it fades from the biblical picture in 2 Samuel 15:7–10, though the city continued to be occupied. Of importance is the fact that it was the

---

95 An article in the *Biblical Archaeological Review* for September/October 2001 by Kenneth Kitchen.

city that David used as his headquarters until he moved to Jerusalem (2 Samuel 2:1–4). It was confidently asserted by some archaeologists that the story of David's monarchy is legend since there is no evidence of Hebron being a fortified city either at the time of Joshua (see Joshua 10:36–37)—which is known as the Late Bronze Age, or in the time of David—which was around 1000 BC and is known as the Iron Age.

However, ancient Hebron was excavated for three summers in the 1960s by Philip Hammond of Princeton Theological Seminary in America, and later by one of his students, Jeffrey Chadwick, who made 'numerous trips to the site'; he supplemented this by conversations with Israeli archaeologists, his own excavations there, and a PhD thesis on his findings. Chadwick concludes, 'The evidence is strong that Hebron was a thriving city in the Late Bronze Age just before the time the Bible says the Israelites captured it … It can certainly be said that nothing excavated at Hebron so far is in any way inconsistent with the Biblical tradition … [at the time of David] Hebron was not only walled and occupied, but judging from finds both inside and outside the wall line, its thriving population seemed to be growing.'[96] It is true that as yet there is no confirmed archaeological evidence of the presence of David himself in Hebron but this is not surprising; there are many kings of the ancient world who are known to us only through the inscriptions that have been left behind.

More evidence from archaeology

THE GENEALOGY OF BEN-HADAD

By the time of the Jewish kings there is no lack of letters and inscriptions from pagan kings of Syria, Assyria and Egypt that confirm the accuracy of the Old Testament history. A stela is a pillar of stone on which a message was chiselled and used as a boundary marker, a tombstone, or a memorial to a military victory. In 1940 a stela of Ben-Hadad was discovered in northern Syria. According to 1 Kings 15:18 Ben-Hadad was 'the son of

---

96 Jeffrey R Chadwick 'The city of the patriarchs slowly yields its secrets', *Biblical Archaeological Review* September/October 2005, pp. 25–33, 70.

Tabrimmon, the son of Hezion, king of Aram (Syria), who was ruling in Damascus'. This is exactly the order that appears on Ben-Hadad's stele.

AHAB'S IVORY PALACE [97]

In addition to being the wife of Ahab, Jezebel was a Phoenician princess, and the Phoenician craftsmen were experts in the art of carving ivory. From the time of King Solomon onwards, ivory was a symbol of wealth, and when the monarchy divided, both Israel and Judah squandered their riches in this way. It was this wasteful luxury that the prophet Amos vigorously condemned in his ministry (see Amos 3:15 and 6:4).

The account of the reign of Ahab, king of Israel, informs us that, 'The palace he built was inlaid with ivory' (1 Kings 22:39). Ruins at Samaria, where Ahab and Jezebel lived, have revealed hundreds of fragments of ivory, and larger items also, many of them intricately carved. These are believed to date from the time of Ahab, about 860 BC. Among the items of tribute that the Assyrian king Sennacherib claims Hezekiah sent to him at Nineveh are 'ivory-decorated beds and ivory-decorated armchairs, elephant hide and tusks...' Critics once questioned the idea of Ahab making an 'ivory palace', but it is now known that the custom was to overlay wood with carved ivory.

THE BLACK OBELISK [98]

Jehu was not of royal descent; he was a soldier who butchered his way to power. Having killed the kings of Israel and Judah, he doubtless felt a little uneasy about some of the enemies he had made. A strong friend and ally would be a wise policy.

In 1845 Austen Henry Layard had just packed his horse and left the site he had been digging on the banks of the River Tigris, when a workman caught up with him and urged him to return; a two metre block of black polished limestone had been found lying in a trench. It was carved with pictures and writing on all four sides. The 'Black Obelisk' (an obelisk is

---

97 *Evidence for the Bible*, p. 49.
98 *Evidence for the Bible*, p. 52.

a shaped block of stone, generally tapering at one end) proved to be a commemoration of the triumphs of the Assyrian king Shalmaneser III. (This is not the king referred to in 2 Kings 17, 18, who is Shalmaneser V.)

Part of the obelisk depicts rulers in national costume bringing tribute to the king. The first panel in the second line shows a kneeling figure in Israelite dress with the inscription: 'Tribute of Yaua, son of Humri: I received silver, gold, a golden bowl, a golden beaker, golden goblets, golden pitchers, lead, a royal staff, a javelin.' This is 'Jehu, son of Jehoshaphat' (2 Kings 9:14). In fact Jehu is the fourth in line of descent from Omri, who was the founder of this dynasty, but at this time Assyrian records referred to Israel as *mat-Humri* ('land of Omri') or *bit-Humri* ('house of Omri'). Behind the kneeling Jehu a line of his servants follow laden with the items of tribute. The inscription does not say that Shalmaneser defeated Jehu in battle, so this looks like a proactive offering on the part of the Israelite king to find an ally!

The story is not ended here, because in order to make a friend of Shalmaneser Jehu abandoned Hazael of Damascus. Hazael is also mentioned in the obelisk, but he had resisted the Assyrian king. For this treachery Jehu and Israel paid dearly in later years, as 2 Kings 10:32 reveals. If the figure on the obelisk is that of Jehu himself, which is most likely, it is the only representation of one of the kings of Israel or Judah from the records of a pagan ruler.

PILATE'S PRIDE[99]

In 1961 a team of archaeologists from Milan were excavating at Caesarea when they came across a partly defaced limestone block with a very significant name on it. The stone had been reused as part of the steps in an ancient theatre. Caesarea was the headquarters of the Roman army of occupation in the time of Jesus and the name on the stone was that of Pilate. We know him as Pontius Pilate, the governor of Judaea who was responsible for condemning Jesus to death (Matthew 27:1–2). All that remained of the inscription was the word 'Tiberieum' in the first line, the

---

99 *Evidence for the Bible*, p. 146.

end of the word 'Pontius' and the whole of 'Pilatus' in the second line, and what is probably the last half of the word ' praefectus' (Prefect) in the third line. It is clearly an inscription by Pilate himself to the fact that he had built a shrine to honour the Emperor Tiberius—the shrine was called Tiberieum.

Pilate wanted everyone to know of his loyal actions to the Emperor, not least the emperor himself, since Pilate was not managing affairs in Judaea very well and was eventually recalled to Rome to answer for his conduct. No one has seriously doubted the existence of Pilate since both the Roman historian, Tacitus (AD 55–117), and the Jewish historian, Josephus (writing his *Antiquities of the Jews* in AD 93), mention him by name in connection with the death of Jesus, but this stone is the only 'hard' evidence of his name in the first century.

These illustrations form only a small sample of the material available today. Hundreds of inscriptions on monuments and tombs, and thousands of letters written on stone or clay tablets are still waiting to be deciphered and translated. Archaeologists are still digging, scholars are still studying. More information comes to light every year.

CONCLUSION

We saw in the previous chapter the valuable contribution that was made to biblical studies by the work of Robert Dick Wilson and William Mitchell Ramsay. With so many more discoveries since their day, it is no longer possible to pretend that the evidence does not exist. Earlier last century, the father of Professor Donald Wiseman, P J Wiseman—himself a traveller and author—claimed that if the mass of evidence available today had been available in the nineteenth century it would have been impossible for the Higher Critics to put forward the views they did.

4. Guidelines for combat

No book has been subject to such intense academic and popular criticism as the Bible, and yet it has always come through unscathed. It has been called 'an anvil that has worn out many hammers.'

The claim that the Bible is inerrant in all its facts and doctrines (plenary inerrancy) and the actual words of the original manuscripts (verbal inerrancy), is not without its challenges. There are parts of the Bible that appear to contain mistakes and inconsistencies. However, the persistent challenge: 'The Bible is full of errors and contradictions' is normally made by those who have only a superficial knowledge of the Bible or a stubborn prejudice against it.

In the next chapter, we will consider some examples of the supposed errors and contradictions, but it will be wise first to consider some of the principles that should control our approach to the subject.

Responding to criticism

IS A BIBLE WITHOUT ERROR NECESSARY?

A not uncommon charge against those who believe in the reliability of the Bible is that it forces its defenders to concentrate on the detail of Scripture at the expense of its message. In reality the very opposite is true. Those who believe in a Bible without error have always been at the forefront of explaining and applying its text and sharing its message across the world through translation, literacy, commentaries, preaching and personal evangelism. The great majority of mission societies that commenced in the nineteenth century were evangelical in their foundation.

The only reason why conservative evangelicals spend time defending the detail of Scripture is because those who have an interest in destroying its truth need to be answered. It is surely better to give a vigorous defence rather than avoid the issue by suggesting that minor errors would not make any difference to our full confidence in an infallible Scripture. The Swiss theologian Karl Barth claimed that the authors of Scripture could be 'at fault in any word, and have been at fault in every word', and yet the writers have still spoken the word of God in their fallible and erring human word.[100] Theologians may understand what that means, but for most ordinary people it stands reason on its head. For Barth, the Bible was not the word of God but it *became* the word of God as it spoke into our lives.

However, so much of the biblical record is vital as a foundation for Christian doctrine. The origin of the universe, the creation of the human race and what went wrong, the foundation of true marriage, the plan of salvation and the way of redemption, are all rooted firmly in what the Scriptures claim to be real history. The unique conception, birth, ministry, death, resurrection and ascension of Jesus are fundamental facts vital to understand who he was and what he came to do. If the other miracles recorded in the Bible cannot be trusted, how can we be sure of these also? In short, can we really have a reliable salvation based upon an unreliable history?

COULD WRITERS RECALL EVENTS ACCURATELY?

For some who read the Bible, it seems impossible that men could accurately record events that happened so long before. Surely, the argument runs, with the passing of time they would have forgotten the details; we can therefore assume that even if the Gospel writers intended to be accurate, they must have suffered from slips of memory. We are then given the imaginary example of four people reporting on the same incident who will each, unintentionally of course, contradict the others. There are two replies to this.

In Book 1 chapter 3 in this series some illustrations of impressive memory recall both in the ancient world and today were given. Those

---

100 Karl Barth, *Church Dogmatics* 1.2 trans G T Thomson and Harold Knight (Edinburgh, T & T Clark, 1956), p. 530.

examples, separated by more than two thousand years, demonstrate how powerfully accurate the human memory can be with sufficient incentive.

However, it should not be overlooked that Jesus promised his disciples that the Holy Spirit would aid their memory and 'remind you of everything I have said to you' (John 14:26). See Book 2 chapter 5 in this series under 'The authority Christ gave to his disciples'. Even if we overlook the vital ingredient of the divine aid to ensure an accurate memory, we can surely expect that the disciples rehearsed the words of their Master over and over again until they could accurately recall his teaching. They were at least convinced of the fact that what Jesus really said was far more valuable than anything they could have invented. In addition, the importance of contemporary writing in the first century should not be overlooked. There is no good reason to doubt that the disciples of Jesus, and others, wrote down some of the teaching of Jesus immediately it was given. See in this series Book 1 chapter 3 (under 'Reading and writing in the first century') and Book 4 chapter 2 (under 'Writing materials for the first manuscripts').

IS INERRANCY REASONABLE?

The doctrine of verbal and plenary inspiration does not depend upon our being able to prove infallibly and conclusively a solution to every question raised, but it does depend upon our being able to demonstrate that no statement of Scripture is, by any and every reasoning, inaccurate. If we can show that there is a reasonable and possible solution of any particular issue, then the doctrine stands intact.

We must abandon our belief only when the Bible is proved, beyond all reasonable doubt and beyond all possible defence, to be found in error. Understanding this important principle led Charles Haddon Spurgeon, the popular nineteenth century preacher in London, to ignore the conclusions of the so-called 'higher critical' scholars who denied as many of the historical facts of the Bible as they possibly could. He knew that if he interpreted the Bible correctly, it would never be proved wrong and that it was the arguments of the critics that would be found false. In this Spurgeon has been vindicated.

LIES AND MORE LIES

A commitment to the full accuracy of Scripture does not mean that every part of Scripture is a proclamation of truth. The Bible records lies told by men and the devil. When David fled from his son Absalom, Hushai deliberately gave poor military counsel against the 'good advice' of Ahithophel to allow David time to escape (2 Samuel 17:14). Years earlier when he was escaping from King Saul, David himself had deliberately lied to the priests in the town of Nob, with terrible consequences (1 Samuel 21). Even an old prophet of God knowingly deceived a young prophet, also with a tragic outcome (1 Kings 13). It is evident that certain statements of Job's friends, although they are accurately recorded, are contrary to truth; God himself confirmed this (Job 42:7). Herod claimed that he wanted to worship Christ (Matthew 2:8) but we know from his later action that he had no such intention. Even the devil himself boldly misused Scripture in his temptations of Jesus.

BY THE PEN OF TWO OR MORE WITNESSES

The greatest significance of the four Gospels recording the life of Jesus Christ is precisely that—there are four of them. A good biblical principle is that any matter should be established by two or three witnesses (Matthew 18:16; 1 Timothy 5:19). By providing four independent witnesses to the life, death and resurrection of Christ (at least five for the resurrection appearances), God has confirmed his word in a remarkable way. Yet still critics of the Bible spend their time trying to discover 'irrefutable' discrepancies, some of which we will answer in the next chapter. When a particular criticism is given a reasonable answer, it is often shrugged off and a new one put forward. On the other hand, if we had only one Gospel record we can be sure that critics would use this as strong evidence against the reliability of the Bible, claiming that we cannot give credibility to a single source. They would, understandably, demand more than one biography for such an important life-story.

In Book 1 chapter 3 (under 'Assessing the evidence') of this series, we considered the value of and evidence for the Gospels as eyewitness accounts (see also Book 3 chapter 6 under 'The four Gospels and Acts'). All that is needed here is to underline the huge significance of four independent accounts. Although scholars have tried to create a source from which at least three must have gained some of their information (source Q; see Book 3 chapter 6 under 'The Synoptic problem'), the similarities in accounts, sometimes identical, may just as logically be accurate reporting. The many small differences are equally evidence of independent reporting. However, there is no reason why they may not have used some common source material; not forgetting that at least two of the four were eyewitnesses of Jesus' three years public ministry.

The differences provide evidence that the Gospel writers often worked independently of each other. Quite possibly there were frequently told stories of the actions and teaching of Christ that went the rounds of the infant churches, but it is unreasonable to assume that those churches had no interest in reading reliable accounts of the life of Christ, or that the apostles had no interest in meeting such a need. When Peter affirmed, 'We [presumably a reference to all the apostles] did not follow cleverly invented stories when we told you about the power and coming of our Lord Jesus Christ, but we were eye-witnesses of his majesty' (2 Peter 1:16), he must have had in mind the record that he had passed on to Mark.

When we consider how quickly after the death (often before the death) of a famous person, a cluster of biographies appears in our own day, it is remarkably odd to imagine that the church was satisfied with no official record of Christ for more than a century. This is precisely why the Old Testament is full of genealogies—lists of names tracing the line back for many generations. We have two independent genealogies of Jesus: Matthew follows the line of descent through Joseph, and Luke through Mary.[101] Genealogies were vitally important credentials.

IS HARMONIZING JUSTIFIED?

Harmonizing is the work of unravelling the dissimilarities of common accounts in such a way that they can be seen to tell the full story. Some

---

101 The debate about whether or not Matthew traces the genealogy through Joseph and Luke through Mary is detailed. A summary of the discussion can be found in William Hendriksen's commentary on Luke 3:23–38 (Banner of Truth, Edinburgh 1979), pp. 221–225.

consider that the need to do this betrays a weakness in the Bible and it would be so much better if there were no 'apparent' contradictions. In response we may comment that many of the supposed contradictions would never be seen as such in any book other than the Bible. The high claim that the Bible makes for itself invites opponents to prove it false. No other book has been subject to such demanding claims and minute inspection, so we need not be embarrassed by the need to harmonize the Bible.

When two honest witnesses stand in a court of law with two stories that do not agree in every detail, it is not immediately assumed that one is lying or that either is wrong; a perfectly reasonable explanation may prove both to be true. Like any witness, the Bible has a right to be trusted until it can be proved false.

Kenneth Kantzer provides an excellent example from his own experience of how two apparently contradictory accounts can have a perfectly reasonable explanation. This is his story: 'Some time ago the mother of a dear friend of ours was killed. We first learned of her death through a trusted mutual friend who reported that our friend's mother had been standing on the street corner waiting for a bus, and had been hit by another passing bus. She was fatally injured and died a few minutes later. Shortly after, we learned from the grandson of the dead woman that she had been involved in a collision, was thrown from the car in which she was riding and was killed instantly. The boy was quite certain of his facts, relayed them clearly, and stated that he had secured his information directly from his mother—the daughter of the woman who had been killed. No further information was forthcoming from either source. Now which would you believe? We trusted both friends, but we certainly could not get the data together. Much later, we were able to seat the mother and grandson in our living room. There we probed for a harmonization. We learned that the grandmother had been waiting for a bus, was hit by another bus, and was critically injured. She had been picked up by a passing car and dashed to hospital, but in haste, the car in which she was being transported to the hospital collided with another car. She was thrown from the car and died instantly. This story from my own experience presents no greater difficulty than that of any recorded in the Gospels.' [102]

That account should be read to all critics of the Gospel records.

Craig Blomberg has shown conclusively that secular historians regularly harmonize ancient and apparently conflicting accounts. The Jewish historian, Josephus, is not always consistent with himself, and the many accounts of the life of Alexander the Great present 'contradictions'. In each case, historians will not assume an error in the records but will frequently attempt to harmonize the various strands. Blomberg quotes one historian who concludes, 'as longs as what Josephus tells us is *possible*, we have no right to correct it' and that since the Josephus' history of the Jewish revolt is the best we have it is 'the one that should stand.' Blomberg provides an interesting example of historians harmonizing conflicting numbers in the different accounts of the size of Alexander's army and concludes, 'Here are two expert, contemporary classicists putting forward the very type of harmonizations that most biblical critics would reject out of hand if they came from Evangelicals.' [103]

PROGRESSIVE REVELATION

Our belief in the sufficiency of Scripture does not imply that any one part is necessarily sufficient by itself. There are stages of revelation. For example, we understand far more fully the plan of salvation by the end of the epistle to the Romans than we do at the close of Deuteronomy. Much of the plan of redemption is hidden in types and symbols, ceremonies and sacrifices. So also, we have a far clearer picture of God's perfect pattern for marriage by the end of the New Testament than by the end of the Old. Again, the plan is there, but it is often concealed by God's concession to the hardness of the human heart and the requirements of the day; for this reason, polygamy is not outlawed in the Old Testament.

---

102 Kenneth S Kantzer, 'Can I really trust the Bible?' in *Tough Questions Christians Ask* (Ed. David Neff, Victor Books 1989).

103 Craig L Blomberg in *Hermeneutics, Authority and Canon* (ed Carson and Woodbridge, IVP Leicester 1986), chapter on 'The Legitimacy and Limitations of Harmonization'. This whole chapter is excellent for the subject of harmonizing but see especially pp. 166–168 on Josephus, and pp. 169–170 on Alexander the Great.

The progress of God's revelation also means that some things are more restricted under the new covenant. The song of Deborah (Judges 5) and some of the psalms praying for punishment upon enemies (Psalm 109) may not be appropriate for a Christian congregation to sing as a curse upon their enemies, even though they contain a timeless truth that those who are the enemies of God, are the enemies of his people also. Jesus discouraged his disciples from copying Elijah (Luke 9:54–56) but this does not condemn Elijah's action. David's method of killing his enemies (2 Samuel 8:2) is not a model for modern military commanders. Clearly, as God revealed more of his character and commands, he expected a higher morality from the nations and especially his chosen people. It is significant how far ahead of its cultural context are the moral demands of the New Testament and, for that matter, the Old also.

This progression also means that no one part of Scripture is sufficient in itself. The complete Bible is an essential unity, with each part building to make the whole. The epistle of James is an important part of Scripture, but standing alone it is not the clearest book to teach the doctrine of justification by faith alone; its significance lies in a different, but complimentary, emphasis. It is the whole Bible that is sufficient, not any one part.

The Master Plan of the Bible was presented in Book 1 chapter 1 of this series, and see also Book 6 chapter 2 under: 'What does the rest of the Bible say about this subject?'

BE PATIENT

The number of alleged errors that are sufficiently serious to require a response are only a tiny fraction of the whole Bible. We have already seen that seemingly unsolvable difficulties have been resolved in the light of modern discoveries and the advance of knowledge. It is therefore perfectly right to claim that time may well resolve issues that remain. The certain knowledge of the Hittites, King David of Israel, King Sargon of Assyria, Crown Prince Belshazzar of Babylon, the city of Nineveh and the census decree of Caesar Augustus, are the more obvious of scores of examples where the one-time silence of history became a voice in the support of biblical accuracy.

THE ACTUAL WORDS OF JESUS

In the recorded teaching of Jesus in the Gospels, there are occasional differences in the reported words he used. Before we assume an error in the reporting, there are a few obvious principles that should be kept in mind.

• There is no reason why Jesus should not have used a variety of words in his teaching, even on the same occasion. If a crowd had been with him for a large part of the day, with many coming and going, he would have repeated much of his instruction by using different words. Any open-air preacher will understand this.

• Jesus would doubtless have used the same illustrations, with variations, on many different occasions. We have only one thousandth part of what Jesus taught and did during his three years of ministry.[104] Perhaps few, if any, of the recorded episodes contain all the words that Jesus spoke on any particular occasion. Each writer therefore placed his emphasis upon a different part of Christ's teaching and, since they are never found to be contradictory, we add each contribution to the whole. Preachers regularly repeat their sermons to different congregations but never in exactly the same words. In Matthew 23:1–39 Jesus gave seven 'woes' to the crowds and in Luke 11:37–53 he gave six 'woes' in the house of a Pharisee. His teaching on prayer, recorded in Matthew 6:5–15 and which included the 'Lord's prayer', was given on a different occasion to the similar teaching and 'Lord's prayer' in Luke 11:1–13.

• The question of different words attributed to Jesus raises the question of how far we can be sure that we have the exact words of Jesus, rather than his authentic voice without necessarily his actual words. It is the difference between what is referred to as *ipsissima verba Jesu* (the precise words of Jesus), and *ipsissima vox Jesu* (the precise voice of Jesus).

---

104 John Wesley, the Methodist evangelist in the eighteenth century, preached fifteen sermons a week. With this as an example, it is hardly likely that Jesus taught publicly for less than twenty hours a week. If so, and if he preached at 130 words a minute, which is a normal lecture speed, then in one year of his public ministry Jesus would have used 8,112,000 words, or twenty-four-and-a-half million in three years. There are only 24,000 in the four Gospels—one thousandth.

The difference may be subtle, but it can be important. Although Jesus doubtless on occasions preached in Greek, especially in the Decapolis on the far side of Galilee where Greek was more common, he probably taught mainly in Aramaic. In this case, we have very few of the actual words of Jesus; all we have in the Gospels are those occasions where the Aramaic is retained even in the Greek Testament: *Talitha, koum* (Mark 5:41), *Eloi, Eloi, lama sabachthani* (Mark 15:34), *Tetelestai* (John 19:30, though most versions give us the English translation), *Mariam* (John 20:16 rendered 'Mary' in most translations, but Jesus used her Aramaic name).

We cannot be reading his actual words (*ipsissima verba*) when he preached in Aramaic, because the disciples recorded his words in Greek and we are reading them in English. However, we are hearing his *authentic voice* if the words used by the disciples exactly express what he said. We may say of a translation: 'Yes, those are the exact words.' It is understood that they are not the *ipsissima verba* but they are exactly what was said, carrying the precise meaning—the *ipsissima vox*.

Since languages cannot always be translated word for word, there are bound to be slight variations between the writers in their accounts of the same event. When the Holy Spirit reminded the disciples of everything Christ had said (John 14:26), he allowed them some liberty of expression whilst at the same time ensuring that they conveyed exactly the meaning of Jesus' words. Variation is not contradiction; if different words are occasionally used to report a saying of Jesus then they all help to give the full meaning of what he said. The definition of 'inspiration' in Book 2 chapter 2 of this series is important to note, and worth repeating:

'The Holy Spirit moved men to write. He allowed them to use their own style, culture, gifts and character, to use the results of their own study and research, to write of their own experiences and to express what was in their mind. At the same time, the Holy Spirit did not allow error to influence their writings; he overruled in the expression of thought and in the choice of words. Therefore, they recorded accurately all that God wanted them to say and exactly how he wanted them to say it, in their own character, style and language. The inspiration of Scripture is a harmony of the active mind of the writer and the sovereign direction of the Holy Spirit to produce God's inerrant and infallible word for the human race.'

An example of the different words used in recording the sermons of Jesus is found In Matthew 6:11 where Jesus taught the disciples to pray: 'Give us today our daily bread…' In Luke 11:3 he taught: 'Give us each day…' The verb 'to give' is a completed form in Matthew and a continuous form in Luke. Similarly Matthew uses the word 'today' whilst Luke uses 'each day'. As noted above, Jesus must often have repeated himself when he was preaching to a 'coming and going' crowd in one location. If so, why should he not vary the emphasis to give the fullest possible meaning to the 'newcomers' arriving in the crowd? No contradiction is involved in a different form. Repetition using a variety of words was a familiar method of instruction in biblical times. It is found frequently in the 'Hebrew parallelism', especially in the Psalms, where the same sense is repeated in different words. What is certain is that in both Gospels we can confidently say, 'These are the words of Jesus', since they are what he actually said and what he intended the Gospel writers to record.

A similar example is found in Matthew 3:11 which refers to John the Baptist *carrying* the sandals of the Messiah, whereas John 1:27 refers to him *untying* them. In this instance, even a superficial glance at the two passages indicates that this refers to separate occasions. Since John was preaching over a period of time, it is evident that he also would repeat himself, and why should he not use different words?

Alternative solutions

To avoid some of the apparent errors or contradictions, various solutions have been offered. There can be truth in each of these, but they must be handled with caution.

ARE THE SOURCES IN ERROR?

The writers of the Bible, and particularly of the Old Testament, used many sources for their material. 1 Chronicles 29:29 refers to the 'records of Nathan and Gad' in addition to the book of Samuel. For more on the many other books mentioned in the Old Testament see Book 1 chapter 6 in this series under 'Official records'. Ezra and Nehemiah contain genealogies, letters of Persian kings and other documents, presumably copies from ancient libraries or archives. In the New Testament, Luke lays claim to careful and diligent search (Luke 1:1–4). It is suggested that these original sources may have contained errors and that when they were copied by the inspired writers of Scripture God did not consider it necessary to correct these defects. Matthew Henry, the wise and spiritual seventeenth century Bible commentator, accepts this argument, and in his comment upon some of the problems found in the genealogy of 1 Chronicles 8:1–32 suggests:

'There was no necessity for the making up of defects, no, nor for the rectifying of the mistakes, of these genealogies by inspiration: it was sufficient that he copied them out as they came to his hand, or so much of them as was requisite to the present purpose.'

However, the question is, are there mistakes of this order? It would not undermine the doctrine of inerrancy to admit that there are, and in the next chapter we shall see that when, for example, Joab reported the result of David's census to the king, the figure may only be an estimate rather than exact. All the Scriptures do is accurately report Joab's numbers. Certainly when we have the text of a letter by a pagan king, as in Ezra 7:11–26, the accuracy is limited to the reporting of that letter. If it was one day discovered beyond doubt that Artaxerxes had eight and not seven advisers (v.14) the error would be the king's and not Ezra's.

Similarly, Claudius Lysias was a little 'economical with the facts' in his letter to the Governor Felix when he suggested he rescued Paul from the mob because 'I had learned that he was a Roman citizen'. The truth was that only after he had arrested, and bound Paul and was about to beat him, he discovered he was a Roman citizen. (Acts 21:33–39; 23:27). Luke simply recorded the letter exactly as it was written.

COPYISTS' ERRORS?

In Book 4 chapters 2 and 3 of this series it was acknowledged that over the years of copying the manuscripts of the Bible, and in spite of the great care of most of the scribes, small errors could find their way into the text. Where one single Hebrew letter can change the number twenty into thirty or a Greek letter can change 'who' into 'he', we may acknowledge a copyist's error. But this must be used with caution.

During Stephen's sermon recorded in Acts 7, the Christian martyr claimed that Jacob came to Egypt with seventy-five souls (v. 14) whereas according to Genesis 46:27 the number was seventy. The sixteenth century Reformer John Calvin considered several possibilities in solving this discrepancy but finally attributed it either to an error by a copyist of the Greek translation of the Old Testament (the *Septuagint*) with which Stephen was familiar, or a copyist of the Greek text of Acts changed Stephen's speech to fit the *Septuagint*. Calvin warns his readers that Paul told us not to be too troubled by genealogies.

In the same passage in Acts 7:16, Stephen recalled that Abraham bought a tomb from the sons of Hamor at Shechem, whereas Genesis 23:9 claims that the patriarch bought the cave of Machpelah from 'Ephron son of Zohar'. This is dismissed by Calvin with the words: 'It is manifest that there is a mistake … Wherefore this place must be amended.'[105] In the next chapter a more satisfactory solution to these two apparent mistakes will be suggested. To admit occasional errors in the copying is one thing, but to allow errors in the original autographs is another.

THE BIBLE AND SCIENCE

Many find difficulty in Scripture because some of its statements appear to be contradicted by modern scientific theories or observation. We must, however, always beware of allowing the interpretations of science, whether theoretical or observed, to become the standard for judging the accuracy of Scripture. A firm belief in the virgin conception of Jesus Christ, his miracles, resurrection, and the fact that in creation God made everything *ex nihilo* (out of nothing), can never depend upon what science can verify. The most that any scientist can say is that it has never been observed.

---

105 *Calvin's Commentaries* (Baker Book House. Grand Rapids MI. 1979). Trans, William Pringle 1848. Vol. VIII, pp. 263–265.

No Christian doubts that God can, and does, intervene in the ordered universe he has made. A great weakness in many supposed scientific conclusions is that people forget that when a scientist says, 'We have never seen this happen and we cannot explain how it happens; therefore, it has never happened,' he is using what we call a *non sequitur*—a conclusion that does not logically follow from the premise. No one, scientist or otherwise, can conclude that a virgin birth, or a resurrection from the dead, or creation out of nothing is impossible; no one knows sufficient about the universe to be certain of this. The most anyone can conclude is, 'I have never seen it happen, I do not know how it could happen and I do not believe it would ever happen.' To conclude 'Therefore it did not happen' is as much a statement of faith as concluding, 'I believe that it did happen'. The same is true of prophecy. Some critics will assume that all fulfilled biblical prophecies were written after the event simply because they do not believe in prophecy. That is not a conclusion of scientific observation—which actually runs in the other direction—but a conclusion based upon a personal non-belief.

To avoid a clash with science it is suggested that the Bible is not a scientific textbook and therefore it does not make scientific statements. Of course it is true that the Bible is not a scientific textbook if by that we mean it does not always describe events in the language of modern science. Had God done so, his revelation would have been unintelligible until the present day, and irrelevant within a century from now. Few medical books published a century ago would be of use to a medical student today. Scientific language, theories and practice are constantly changing.

However, it is a fact that the Bible does make claims about subjects that are of great interest to the scientist. The origin of the universe and the description of a universal flood are two examples. The Bible describes both of these in a plain straightforward manner, and in language that every generation can understand. All these are facts capable, in some measure, of scientific investigation. Miracles are not so easily open to scientific investigation and in this sense, they may be 'unscientific'. However, that does not make them against or contrary to science, unless, that is, we make a god of 'scientism'—a belief in the infallibility of scientific observation.

Science, by its very definition, can never reach a final statement. It must always be ready to alter course when new facts demand such action. Revelation, on the other hand, is final. We would therefore expect science, as it advances in knowledge, constantly to change and increasingly to support biblical statements.

It is not the place here to consider the supposed scientific problems in biblical creation as described in the opening chapters of Genesis. These issues are adequately dealt with in a whole range of excellent publications today.[106] The most any scientist should claim is that many scientists *believe* the Bible to be wrong; however, honesty demands the rejoinder that many scientists do *not* think so. Counting the number of scientists on one side or the other proves nothing. We are continually learning of the considered opinion of the majority of 'experts' that has subsequently been overturned. On the premise that there is a God who has revealed himself, it is hardly foolish to believe that revelation is more certain than science.

On this subject, there are some accounts in the Bible that have given critics an opportunity to dismiss its relevance.

THE LANGUAGE OF THE BIBLE

Such expressions as 'the four corners of the earth' (Isaiah 11:12 ESV; NIV has 'quarters') and the 'pillars' of the earth (Psalm 75:3) supposedly reflect a primitive view that the earth was flat, square and supported by posts. Pictures are drawn in text books to illustrate the simplistic Hebrew view. If this is so, it should at once be acknowledged that 'the circle of the earth' (Isaiah 40:22), and Job's claim that God 'spreads out the northern skies over empty space; and suspends the earth over nothing' (Job 26:7), and Elihu's observation that, 'He draws up the drops of water, which distil as rain to the streams; the clouds pour down their moisture and abundant showers fall on mankind' (Job 36:27,28), are statements full of modern scientific understanding.

---

106 See, for example, the publications of Creation Ministries International (CMI), Answers in Genesis (AIG) and Biblical Creation Trust (BCT). See also Stuart Burgess and Andy McIntosh, *Wonders of Creation—design in a fallen world* (Day One Publications, Leominister 2017).

It is wiser to take these statements as poetic descriptions. Interestingly, although hardly surprising, that critics refer to those first two phrases and generally ignore the last three.

STRANGE INCIDENTS

Balaam's donkey speaking (Numbers 22:28), Moses and the Israelites crossing the Red Sea (Exodus 14:21–22), Elisha's floating axe-head (2 Kings 6:6) and Jonah's big fish (Jonah 1:17) are all too absurd for many to accept. But what a man may think absurd is hardly a standard for judging the facts. Perhaps Balaam, Moses, Elisha and Jonah would have considered it absurd to be told that man would one day walk on the moon, be suspended in space a hundred miles above the surface of the earth, sit in a metal tube to fly through the sky at unimaginable speeds, or to live in a similar construction for weeks at the bottom of the ocean—even Jonah did not experience that! In fact an all-powerful God can do what he wants and use whatever means he chooses. It is not science that dismisses any of these events, but a strong faith in unbelief.

JOSHUA'S LONG DAY

Perhaps few stories in the Bible have been so quickly dismissed as untrue as that of the sun standing still, recorded in Joshua 10:12–14. According to our present scientific knowledge of the universe, if the sun appeared to stand still this must mean that the earth had stopped its rotation round the sun and, as a consequence, the earth would be drawn into the sun and burn up. This account is therefore dismissed as impossible.

Is this no more than a poetic story? Joshua is a book written as plain history, and this account is written in that context with no clue that it is not intended to be taken literally. Perhaps it was merely a day so full of activity that to Joshua and his army it seemed that the sun had stopped. Even today we talk about 'time standing still'. However, this response does not take into account all that happened on that day. Here is a brief survey of the events of Joshua 10.

Joshua was compelled by his treaty of peace to help the Gibeonites when they were attacked by five kings of the Amorites. He wanted to gain a complete victory, and to do this required careful strategy and plenty of time. Joshua acted quickly and marched his army through the night from Gilgal to Gibeon, a distance of about 40 km (25 mi) on a 914 m (3,000 ft) ascent. The five kings panicked and fled on the road to Beth Horon. On this road God rained great hailstones on the retreating army, but Joshua's men, tired after a night's hard march and a morning battle, required more time to catch up with the retreating Amorites. The hailstones halted the enemy and gave Joshua's men a much-needed rest; it is unlikely they returned to Gilgal at this point, and v. 15 probably refers to the close of this long day. Having cut off their retreat into Jerusalem, Joshua drove the Amorites a further 26 km (17 mi) to Makkedah where the five kings were discovered hiding in a cave. Joshua sealed the cave and pressed on to Azekah, a further 5 km (3 mi) before returning to deal with the kings at Makkedah, and destroying the city itself (v. 28). At sunset Joshua was at Makkedah with his weary but victorious army (v. 27).

In one full night and a full day, Joshua had marched his men 40 km up a 914 m ascent, fought a battle, chased the retreating enemy a further 40 km to Azekah, returned 5 km to Makkedah and destroyed a city. We may compare this achievement with that of Sir Archibald Hunter who, when he set out to relieve the British Army at Mafeking in South Africa, in May 1900, started at four in the morning, marched his army until eight at night and covered 48 km (30 mi) in those sixteen hours. Perhaps a closer parallel is the fact that a thousand years after Joshua, in 58 BC Julius Caesar claimed that he marched four legions at an incredible 144 km (90 mi) a day for eight days to Geneva and fought a battle against the Helveti at the end.[107] The Roman legionary was not infrequently driven to cover 35 km (22 mi) in five hours and with a full pack weighing 30 kg (70 lbs). For him, a forced march was well in excess of 50 km (33 mi) a day.

It is clear that the story of Joshua 10 demands a longer than usual day. An extra twelve hours would be sufficient—just. We cannot suggest the writer put all the details in to support a pretended miracle, because if this had been his intention he would have given us the distances between

---

107 Michael Grant, *Caesar* (George Weidenfeld and Nicolson Ltd. London 1974), p. 62.

towns and the height of Beth Horon above Gilgal; in fact we have to study carefully the passage, and the geography of the land, in order to realize just how much was achieved in one day.

Explanations of what actually happened in this miracle are numerous. There is no necessity to demand that the earth slowed in its rotation or wobbled on its axis; there are many other ways that God could have supernaturally lengthened daylight over a small part of the earth, just as he brought an unexplained darkness over the land of Israel at the time of the death of Jesus Christ. The phrase in Joshua 10:13 that 'the sun stood still, and the moon stopped' are not necessarily literal events but this is how they appeared to Joshua. Meteorologists today still refer to sunrise and sunset. Despite ancient stories from Egypt, China, New Zealand and Mexico of a long day, there is no need to assume that the whole earth experienced a long day, nor is it necessary to explain how the daylight was lengthened for Joshua. The most straightforward explanation is that God created sufficient light for the Israelites to accomplish their mission. Whatever the 'mechanics' of that day, it was clearly a miracle—but no more so than the resurrection of Christ from the tomb on the third day.

It will be important to keep the principles of this chapter in mind as we turn to consider some examples of supposed errors and contradictions.

5 Solving the problems

Those who ransack the Scriptures to discover errors and contradictions often fail to realise that all their criticisms have been confronted and answered throughout the history of the church by able scholars.

When people assume that the Bible is full of contradictions, few of them have seriously read the book they condemn. However, for the apparent contradictions and errors in the Bible that may not have a wholly satisfactory explanation, the *non sequitur* referred to in the previous chapter must not be forgotten. No one should say, 'This looks like an error; as yet we do not have a perfect explanation, therefore it is an error.' We have already seen in chapters 2 and 3 that time has frequently provided final solutions to once mystifying problems: recall the Hittites, David, Sargon, Belshazzar and Nineveh.

It is now time to turn attention to some supposed errors. For convenience, the subject will be divided into four areas with a few examples for each: dates, numbers and family trees, supposed historical errors, contradictions, and Gospel differences.

Dates, numbers and family trees

It is claimed that in the Bible there are many chronological, numerical and genealogical inaccuracies—in other words, incorrect dates, numbers and family trees.

There are a large number of lists in the Old Testament, but do they have any relevance and are they to be trusted? In biblical times, genealogies in particular were extremely important not merely as historical records, but to establish relationships and the right to hold office; their accuracy therefore mattered in Old Testament society. One example is found in Ezra 2:61–63 where a group of priests 'searched for their family records but could not find them and so were excluded from the priesthood as unclean.' Records were kept by the prophets (2 Chronicles 12:15) and this indicates the importance of the task. However, we have to be aware of the fact that sometimes gaps occur in these list. This is not evidence of error, nor is it unusual. Outside the Bible, the family tree of King Esarhaddon, the king of Assyria and Babylon who is mentioned in 2 Kings 19:37, leaves out no fewer than sixty-two generations.

There are a number of problems with some of these lists, not all of which may be adequately solved.

DAVID COUNTING THE PEOPLE

The record of Joab's census of the fighting men in Israel and Judah shows a difference of nearly a quarter of a million in the lists given in 2 Samuel 24:9 and 1 Chronicles 21:5. In Samuel the number was 800,000 in Israel plus 500,000, in Judah, whereas in Chronicles the number 'who could handle a sword' was 1,100,000 in Israel including 470,000 in Judah. The total number recorded in Samuel is significantly higher.

First, according to 1 Chronicles 27:24, Joab did not complete his count, and his incomplete numbers were 'not entered in the book of the annals of King David.' This is because Joab knew that the king should never have ordered a census and he therefore carried out the order reluctantly and half-heartedly. This could account for the lower figure in Chronicles.

Secondly, according to 1 Chronicles 21:6, Joab did not include the tribes of Levi and Benjamin in the census 'because the king's command was repulsive to him.' Presumably this is why Chronicles records that the numbers were incomplete. Therefore it is likely that the larger figure in Samuel includes an estimate for these two tribes and that the figure in Chronicles ignores these two tribes altogether.

In either case, the figures are simply those given by Joab, with or without the estimate for Levi and Benjamin, and they need not be exact. The accuracy of the Bible extends only to the fact that these were the figures offered to the king; one would be the incomplete list of Joab and the other the official list, perhaps inflated to impress the king.

DAVID'S FAMINE

As a punishment for numbering the people, David was offered, among other choices, 'three years' of famine (1 Chronicles 21:12). But the Hebrew text of 2 Samuel 24:13 refers to 'seven years' where the Greek translation (the *Septuagint*) of this verse has 'three'. 'Three' is the most likely since the other choices were three months of exile or three days of plague. So why does the Hebrew have seven years in Samuel and three years in Chronicles?

Perhaps the solution is to be found in 2 Samuel 21:1. David had already suffered three successive years of crop failure, the results of which would continue into the fourth year; the new period of three years would follow upon this, making a total of seven lean years. Since Chronicles does not mention the earlier famine there is no need for it to add those years to the proposed three. In this case, both texts would be an accurate account.

SOME SCRIBAL ERRORS

We noted in the previous chapter that there are occasions where it is not wrong to plead that a small error which has found its way into the text during the centuries of copying and recopying is sufficient to account for a difference. The number of possible copyist's errors is extremely small. A copyist's mistake never involves any major area of the biblical record; all the instances are in small details of numbers or an occasional word; mostly they are confined to the books of Samuel, Kings and Chronicles where we can cross-check with a similar passage in Scripture. In Book 4 chapter 2 of this series under 'copying the Old Testament', the difficulty of copying words that have no vowels or punctuation was noted. It can be readily appreciated how easily an occasional mistake could have been made; in most instances just one letter can make a difference. Here are a few examples of copyist's errors.

- 1 Kings 4:26 and 2 Chronicles 9:25 both claim that Solomon had 12,000 horsemen, but whereas Chronicles speaks of 4,000 stalls for horses and chariots, Kings has the unusually large figure of 40,000. This figure is almost certainly incorrect, particularly since 1 Kings 10:26 refers to

Solomon possessing 1,400 chariots which would be a reasonable figure to require 4,000 stalls for chariots and horses, allowing two horses to each chariot. In modern Hebrew 40,000 becomes 4,000 by writing the letter *mem* in place of the letter *he* and they are very similar letters. In modern Hebrew *mem* is like this מ, and *he* is like this ה. Such a small mistake is easy to understand, and in reading his text back, a scribe might well have read what he expected to see rather than what he had actually written—something we are all familiar with.

- In 1 Kings 5:13–16 and 2 Chronicles 2:2, there are eight figures quoted in these passages (five in Kings and three in Chronicles); of these, two are mentioned only in Kings, two more are mentioned in both and agree exactly, the last one is mentioned in both, but Kings has 3,300 while Chronicles has 3,600. Again, the difference between these two figures is the omission of the single Hebrew letter *lamed*. Since 2 Chronicles 2:18 repeats the 3,600, that is most likely to be the correct figure.

- In 1 Kings 9:28 and 2 Chronicles 8:18, the difference between the '420 talents of gold' from Ophir and the 450 talents, is the difference between two very similar letters in the Hebrew. The numeral for 20 is כ and for 50 it is נ.

- 2 Kings 24:8 is correct in giving the age of Jehoiachin as eighteen years when he came to the throne. But in 2 Chronicles 36:9 his age is given as eight years (though some translations, including the *New International Version*, correct this to eighteen). Just one word has dropped out to cause this error, and it is an understandable error because the word following the one that is missing is similar in appearance; the scribe's eye must have run along the line a little too fast.

- According to the Hebrew text in 1 Samuel 13:5 the unsustainable number of 30,000 chariots is attributed to the Philistine army; no number remotely close to this has ever been recorded in ancient warfare. However, in the same context, we are informed that there were 'six thousand charioteers' and the number of charioteers always exceeds the number of chariots. Some manuscripts of the *Septuagint* (the Greek translation of the Old Testament [108]) change the number of chariots to 3,000 (this allows two men to a chariot—a driver and an archer). This requires changing just one Hebrew letter—doubtless another small scribal error. For this reason, many translations follow the *Septuagint* text and read 3,000.

In each of these examples we have been able to correct the scribal error by the Scripture itself; although we cannot always do this.

ORNAN'S THRESHING-FLOOR

There is a great difference between the 'fifty shekels of silver' in 2 Samuel 24:24 and the 'six hundred shekels of gold' in 1 Chronicles 21:25 that King David paid to Araunah. However, the first refers only to the price David paid for the 'threshing floor and the oxen' while the second refers to the price he paid for the 'site', that is the whole area of Mount Moriah; this was several acres in extent and the temple was later built on it (1 Chronicles 22:1). This is an example of the importance of reading the texts carefully before arriving at a wrong conclusion.

THE KINGS OF ISRAEL AND JUDAH

There are differences in the total period covered by the kings of Israel and Judah if we simply add up separately the individual years of the kings. The issue of resolving the seeming discrepancies in the length of the reigns of the biblical kings has challenged the minds of many Old Testament scholars over the years and some have concluded that any solution is impossible and that the numbers are hopelessly untrustworthy. However, it should be kept in mind that chronologies were carefully and accurately recorded and preserved in Bible times. According to 2 Chronicles 12:15 the records were kept by 'Shemaiah the prophet and Iddo the seer that deal with genealogies.' This was a significant profession entrusted to skilled men. Clearly the records were not documented in a sloppy or casual fashion.

---

108 For the *Septuagint* see Book 4 chapter 2 in this series.

Edwin Thiele has painstakingly researched this subject and offers many convincing solutions to the issue. He concludes 'Today, I believe the problem to be basically solved.'[109] Among his resolution of the apparent discrepancies are the following points:

- In Israel, the month of a king's accession to the throne (the regnal year) was reckoned from the spring, whereas in Judah it was reckoned from the autumn. This meant that in Israel the regnal year overlapped into two years and a king coming to the throne in the summer would be starting his reign in the fifth regnal year of a king in Judah.

- In addition, a king might reckon his regnal year as the year he began his reign or from the first full year after his accession. There is evidence of both systems used among the Jewish monarchs and the surrounding nations.

- A third point is that the kings of Judah and Israel often used their own system of reckoning to describe the reign of the other nation; in this case the two figures are unlikely to coincide.

- Frequently the years are rounded up to the nearest year, so that a king who died in his fortieth year, even if only one month into it, would often be said to have reigned forty years.

- More significantly, kings would often establish their son/successor as a co-regent and therefore the length of the successor's reign might be reckoned from the coregency or the full reign. Evidently a significant part of Manasseh's long reign of fifty-five years was his co-regency with his father who had been ill to the point of death (2 Kings 20:1). Putting 'his house in order' would necessitate Hezekiah planning for the future monarch by setting up Manasseh as co-regent, but in the event, Hezekiah had another fifteen years to reign (v.6).

---

109 Edwin R Thiele, *A Chronology of the Hebrew Kings* (The Zondervan Corporation, Grand Rapids, Michigan 1978). The whole discussion is detailed and elaborate and a careful study of Thiele is needed to grasp the significance of his conclusions. Thiele presented his views first in 1944 and again in *The Mysterious Numbers of the Hebrew Kings* (University of Chicago Press, Chicago 1965).

Another co-regency is when both Amaziah and Azariah were kings in Judah; the length of Amaziah's reign is given as twenty-nine years in 2 Kings 14:2 whilst Azariah's reign is given as fifty-two years in 2 Kings 15:2. The total is not eighty-one years because Azariah overlapped the twenty-nine years of Amaziah.[110] During the period of the kings there were nine coregencies, one being when Israel had two opposing kings, Tibni and Omri (1 Kings 16:21). This overlap illustrates, according to Thiele, a 'dual dating' method.[111]

Therefore, some differences within Scripture can be explained simply by alternative methods of calculating the length of a reign. This variety presents a problem even for historians studying non biblical kings. Cyrus took the throne of Persia in 559 BC although his father, Cambyses I, did not die until 551 BC. Even when Cyrus became king, Astyages was in control of Media and not until 550 BC could Cyrus claim the whole empire. So, when did his reign begin? Cicero claims that Cyrus of Persia reigned thirty years; Ptolemy allows him only nine years from his defeat of Babylon; whilst Xenophon reduces this to seven years from the time Cyrus became sole monarch. Perhaps Ezra's dating (Ezra 1:1) is based upon this last approach, commencing his reign when Cyrus became the sole and undisputed king.

Edwin Thiele has, at the very least, provided a persuasive and reasonable explanation for the apparent discrepancies in the length of the monarchies recorded in the Bible. No one can accept errors in this area before they have mastered Thiele's analysis and responded to it.

Note: It is possible to fix accurately the dates of some Hebrew kings by comparison with the known dates of Assyrian kings, which the Assyrian's fixed by astronomical observations. For example, Assyrian records date the battle of Qarqar in the sixth year of Shalmaneser III; this would be 853 BC. In this battle, he fought a consortium of kings which, his record claims, included Ahab of Israel. In the eighteenth year of Shalmaneser

---

110 Thiele analyses all nine of these overlapping monarchies, pp. 23–28.
111 Thiele, pp. 33–64.

he claims to have received tribute from Jehu of Israel which would be 841 BC.[112] That at least places parameters for Ahab and Jehu.

THE GENEALOGY OF JESUS

Some family lists are not intended to be complete. The genealogy of Jesus recorded in Matthew is grouped in three lots of fourteen. This reflects a tidy style but does not necessarily claim to be complete. When Matthew said Uzziah was born to Jehoram (Matthew 1:8) he knew perfectly well, for his Old Testament told him, that Ahaziah, Joash and Amaziah came in between; in the Hebrew mind, descendants were born to their ancestors, however many generations lay between. Matthew's list differs from Luke's only in this, that Matthew traces Jesus' descent through David to Joseph, the male and therefore the legal line. Luke traces it through Nathan to Mary, the natural line. Both are accurate, but the purpose of each is different. Incomplete family lists in Scripture are thoughtlessly taken as examples of errors, but those lists are not necessarily intended to be complete.

The statement that one man was father of another may leave out many generations in between. One example among many is in 2 Kings 22:2, where Josiah is said to have walked 'in all the ways of his father David', however, Josiah was the sixteenth generation from David and the writer of the book of Kings was well aware of this fact. Such deliberate shortening of lists is quite common even outside the Bible. There is no distinct Hebrew word for 'grandson' (or grandfather) and therefore the only way to refer to a grandson many times removed was either to give all the fathers that came between or miss them all out and call him 'son'.

GOSPEL CHRONOLOGY

The different order of the accounts recorded in the Gospels would only present a problem if each writer claimed to give the exact order. When Luke promised to provide 'an orderly account' (Luke 1:3), the word

---

112 For both these records see Anderson and Edwards, *Evidence for the Bible* (Day One Publications, Leominster 2014), pp. 51–52.

means no more than 'with a meaningful order'. The Gospel writers chose to arrange their material according to their individual purpose; they sometimes grouped together episodes or parables that fitted a theme. In this sense they were 'redactors', or editors.

Luke, for example, gathers a cluster of events and teaching from chapters 11 to 17, and such statements as 'One day Jesus was praying in a certain place' (11:1) could be anytime and anywhere during his ministry. Even the statement in 17:11 that he was, 'on his way to Jerusalem … along the border between Samaria and Galilee', may cover only the events of the following eight verses.

The accusation of the Pharisees that Jesus cast out demons by Beelzebub, which is recorded in Matthew 12 and Luke 11, may have been a different occasion to that recorded in Mark 3:20–30; it is very likely that the Pharisees made this accusation on more than one occasion and his reply would have been much the same. Similarly, the seven 'woes' against the Pharisees recorded in Matthew 23:1–39 were spoken to 'the crowds and his disciples' whilst the six 'woes' recorded in Luke 11:37–53 were given in the house of a Pharisee.

For this reason, any attempt to piece together an exact sequence for the events and teaching of the three years of Jesus' public ministry will always prove an impossible and inaccurate task. The most that is useful is to gather the same events or teaching together for the purpose of filling out the full account. Such a synopsis has been attempted in Book 6 chapter 5 of this series.

NUMBERS ON THE DAY OF PENTECOST

It had been assumed by critical commentators that the numbers recorded in Acts for the people converted on the day of Pentecost (Acts 2:41 and 4:4) were unreal and exaggerated to suit the extravagant claims of the compiler of Acts. One writer concludes that such a high number as 5,000 converts are, 'of course an unreal figure, which can in no way be brought into accordance with the actual situation', and others that it is 'a greatly exaggerated figure.'[113] It was thought that the population of Jerusalem was little more than twenty-five thousand at this time and therefore such numbers were out of all proportion to the size of the city, and it would not be possible to speak to such large numbers without the aid of amplification. This last reason reveals ignorance of the fact that history records far greater numbers addressed at one time.[114]

Significantly, recent detailed research concludes that the population of Jerusalem in the first century would have been between sixty to one hundred and twenty thousand, with estimates that this was doubled by the number of pilgrims in the city at Passover.[115] Some commentators still use the worn-out arguments of earlier critics.

Historical errors?

One by one details that previously were assumed to be historical errors have been found to be accurate, as we have seen in previous chapters. Unfortunately, despite the constant vindication of biblical records, some critics continue to insist that it is an unreliable record. Here are two examples, reflecting the accuracy of Jesus' words.

'ABIATHAR THE HIGH PRIEST'

Mark 2:26 quotes Jesus as asserting, 'In the days of Abiathar the high priest, he [David] entered the house of God and ate the consecrated bread.' This was at the time of David's visit to the city of Nob. 1 Samuel 21:1 names the priest as Ahimelech. He is not actually called the 'high priest' in Samuel, though we may assume that he was. Was Jesus mistaken?

---

113 *The Book of Acts in its First Century Setting*, Vol 4. *In its Palestinian Setting* ed. Richard Bauckham (William B Eerdmans Publishing Company, Grand Rapids Michigan 1995), chapter 8 'The Population Size of Jerusalem and the Numerical Growth of the Jerusalem Church.' Wolfgang Reinhardt, p. 238, where these quotations are referenced though not endorsed.

114 In 1742 the evangelist George Whitefield preached to 20,000 at Moorfields in London and this was not unusual. On the occasion of the Indian Mutiny in October 1857, the Victorian preacher, C H Spurgeon, is known to have preached at the Crystal Palace in London, without any amplification, to no less than 23,654 people; they passed though turnstiles so the figure is exact.

115 As above, *The Book of Acts*, pp. 238–265.

We know that Ahimelech's son, Abiathar, was with his father at this time and later was the only survivor of Saul's massacre of the priests of Nob (1 Samuel 22:20). Abiathar certainly became high priest on his father's death and may have been acting jointly with his elderly father at the time of David's visit. There would be nothing unusual in such an arrangement. Whether or not Abiathar was joint high priest at the time, Jesus' statement is perfectly correct in that the episode did take place 'in the days of Abiathar' who later became the high priest in the time of David (1 Samuel 30:7).

A similar situation arises in the New Testament when Luke speaks of both Annas and Caiaphas as high priest (Luke 3:2 and Acts 4:6), and John does the same (John 18:13,19,24). In fact Annas had been deposed by the Romans in AD 15 and his son-in-law Caiaphas took the office. According to Jewish tradition the office of high priest was for life and thus even if he was deposed or functioned jointly with his successor, his title was retained.

'ZECHARIAH THE SON OF BEREKIAH'

A more complex issue is Jesus' reference to the murder of 'Zechariah, the son of Berekiah' (Matthew 23:35). This appears to contradict 2 Chronicles 24:20 where he is called 'Zechariah, the son of Jehoiada'. Was Jesus referring to the 'Zechariah son of Berekiah, the son of Iddo' who preached at the time of Nehemiah (Zechariah 1:1). This is unlikely because there is no reference either in the Old Testament or in Jewish tradition to the death of the Zechariah in the time of Nehemiah.

So did Jesus make a mistake in calling Zechariah 'the son of Berekiah'? Was he confusing the two men? No Jew, whether Jesus or the Gospel writer Matthew, would make an obvious blunder like this. It has been suggested that a scribe, copying out the text of Matthew, remembered the Zechariah son of Berekiah and erroneously inserted the name here. This is also most unlikely since virtually every Greek manuscript of this verse that we possess contains the words 'son of Berekiah'. The fact that only one old copy of *Codex Sinaiticus* omits these words shows how careful the copyists were with their texts. So, who is this Zechariah that Jesus referred to?

The same reference in Luke 11:51 reads, '...from the blood of Abel to the blood of Zechariah who perished between the altar and the temple.' There is no reference here to Zechariah's father, and it is most natural to take this as a reference to the first and last of the recorded Old Testament martyrs. Clearly, Jesus is referring to the Zechariah of 2 Chronicles 24, so why does he refer to him as 'the son of Berekiah'?

Several suggestions have been offered, including a reference in the apocryphal *Infancy Gospel of James* to a priest named Zachariah who was murdered in the Temple, and a reference in Josephus to the assassination by the Jews of a godly citizen named 'Zacharius, son of Baruch'.[116] But this took place over three decades after the death of Jesus. Others suggest that the 'you killed' in Matthew 23 refers to the actual Pharisees in front of Jesus and to an act of assassination that they would be aware of, but of which secular history is now silent. This is not impossible, especially in the light of the reference in Josephus to a similar act that is undisputed; however, it is unlikely that such a flagrant breach of the holy place would have gone unrecorded.

Significantly, when referring to the murder of Zechariah in 2 Chronicles, the Jewish *Targum of Lamentations* refers to the murder of Zechariah as the son of Iddo:

'Is it fitting to murder in the House of the Sanctuary of the Lord the priest and the prophet, as you murdered Zechariah the son of Iddo, the high priest and faithful prophet, in the House of the Sanctuary of the Lord on the Day of Atonement, because he admonished you not to do that which was evil before the Lord?'[117]

There is no doubt that this is a reference to the Zechariah of Chronicles, and no one suggests an error in the Targum. Is 'Iddo' a shortened form of Jehoiada or the grandfather of Jehoiada? Later, the Targum refers to this Zechariah as 'the king's son-in-law', which is exactly who the Jehoiada of 2 Chronicles 24:20 was according to 2 Chronicles 22:11. So, the Jews

---

116 Josephus, *Wars*, Book 4.5:4.
117 *The Targum of Lamentations*, Book 2:20, Trans. Philip S Alexander (Liturgical Press, Collegeville, MN, 2007), pp. 140–141. The *Targum* was written around 587 BC.

understood Jehoiada as also having the name Iddo? Why could not the Berekiah of Jesus' reference be a family name also?

We have already noted that there is no distinct Hebrew word for 'grandson', and if the Zechariah of Chronicles was in fact the grandson of Jehoiada—which is quite likely since 2 Chronicles 24:15 tells us that Jehoiada died at the age of 130 years—it would be natural for Chronicles to refer to them as father and son. An example of this is found in a statement of the other Zechariah. He calls himself 'the son of Berekiah, son of Iddo' (Zechariah 1:1) while in Ezra 5:1 and 6:14 he is called simply 'the son of Iddo' (*New International Version* 'descendant'); in fact, he was the grandson of Iddo. It is quite possible that Ezra used this term 'son of Iddo' to avoid confusion with the other Zechariah in Chronicles whose father was also a man by the name of Berekiah.

None of the above can finally resolve the issue, but it does make clear that there are possible and reasonable factors, of which we are not aware, that would indicate that the 'error' was more apparent than real. Certainly, neither the Pharisees nor the Gospel writer saw any need to correct the statement of Jesus.

Contradictions?

Our claim that the Bible never contradicts itself even though compiled by some forty different writers over a period of fifteen hundred years is, understandably, challenged. A few examples are given here of where it is assumed that we have all the information in the biblical narrative. This is a false assumption. The Bible was not written to answer critics, it is presenting the outline of events that may have contained thousands of details that are not given; these details could well account for events that would clarify the text. For example, a thoughtless criticism is the suggestion that since Exodus 9:6 records the death of 'all the livestock of the Egyptians', none could have remained to be killed in verse 19. Either the word 'all' in verse 6 is a general term which does not mean all without a single exception or, more likely, the Egyptians, having lost their animals, raided the land of Goshen and plundered the Israelite herds.

Chapter 5

PROBLEMS IN DEUTERONOMY

Scholars who deny that Moses was the author of the Pentateuch emphasize minor differences between the laws in Deuteronomy and those in Leviticus and Numbers. The laws on tithes differ in Deuteronomy 12:6,17–19; 14:22–29; 26:12–15 from Numbers 18:21–31. The most straightforward reconciliation is that we have in Deuteronomy a 'second tithe' different from the first and to be given in different circumstances.

There are small differences in the laws governing firstlings (compare Deuteronomy 15:19–20 with Numbers 18:17–18), bondservants (compare Deuteronomy 15:12–18 with Exodus 21:1–6) and eating carrion (compare Deuteronomy 14:21 with Leviticus 17:15). But when read carefully, none of these presents a contradiction, they are easily reconciled as additions and small changes to previous laws in the light of a changed situation. Deuteronomy was preparing the people for the settlement in the promised land of Canaan, whereas previous laws were concerned with the wilderness wanderings.

GOLIATH AND HIS BROTHER

1 Chronicles 20:5 informs us that in renewed fighting between Israel and the Philistines, during the reign of David: 'Elhanan the son of Jair killed Lahmi the brother of Goliath'; this Goliath is probably the giant David had killed as recorded in 1 Samuel 17. But 2 Samuel 21:19 omits the words, 'Lahmi the brother of', and the suggestion is that Elhanan killed Goliath himself. However, since the writer of Samuel has already recorded the death of Goliath (1 Samuel 17) he is unlikely to have forgotten this or to expect his readers to have done so. There are two possible explanations. The first is that the Philistine word 'goliath' may simply mean 'giant'; in this case the writer of Samuel having already spoken of the Goliath whom David killed, is content in 2 Samuel 21:19 to refer to this man as 'a goliath' knowing that the two will not be confused. The writer of Chronicles, on the other hand, has not previously spoken of Goliath and therefore must be more careful to avoid confusion.

WHO INCITED DAVID?

2 Samuel 24:1 records that 'the LORD' incited David to the disobedient action of counting the people of Israel. 1 Chronicles 21:1 speaks of Satan inciting him. Which is correct? This is a theological rather than a textual matter; it is only a failure to understand the relationship between the sovereign God and the work of Satan that causes a problem at this point. In 2 Corinthians 12:7–8 Paul speaks of the 'thorn in my flesh, a messenger of Satan', which he clearly saw as coming from the Lord. God's judgement or correction is sometimes seen when he allows Satan a limited 'free hand'. This whole issue is exactly what we find in the first chapter of Job.

WAR BETWEEN ASA AND BAASHA

1 Kings 15:16,32 state clearly that there was war between these two kings 'throughout their reigns'. But 2 Chronicles 15:19 claims: 'There was no more war until the thirty-fifth year of Asa's reign.' It is likely that the difference lies in the use of the word 'war'. Although Israel under Baasha, and Judah under Asa, were constantly in a condition of threats and hostility, there was no major armed conflict until the thirty-fifth year of Asa's reign. Even today we use the term 'war' to cover both sustained but isolated guerrilla attacks and a full-scale military clash between two or more nations. In fact, 1 Kings 15:17 tells us what was happening at this time: Baasha laid siege to Judah, preventing 'anyone from leaving or entering the territory'. Evidently there were no pitched battles and no declarations of war; instead there was an uneasy peace during which Baasha contained the movements of his southern neighbours.

PAUL'S TESTIMONY

Sometimes a less than careful translation can mislead us. In Acts 9:7 we are informed that when Paul saw a great light and heard the voice of Jesus, those accompanying him on the road to Damascus 'heard the sound but did not see anyone.' In his own testimony recorded in Acts 22:9 Paul maintained that they 'did not hear the voice of him who spoke to me' (*New King James Version*). A more accurate translation at this point would dispel the problem. The verb 'to hear' when followed by the accusative case may be taken to mean 'to understand'; and so it should be translated 'My companions saw the light, but they did not understand the voice.' (NIV/ESV). In Acts 9, with the genitive case, they heard the sound of the voice, but in Acts 22 with the accusative case we are informed that they did not understand the voice.

PAUL'S OLD TESTAMENT HISTORY

Paul claimed in 1 Corinthians 10:8 that 23,000 died 'in one day' of the plague, whereas Numbers 25:9 refers to the number of dead as 24,000. Paul may well have been making an allowance for the leaders who were killed by the sword of the judges (see Numbers 25:4–5); presumably these were killed before the plague broke out and 23,000 died of the plague in one day. Numbers 25:9, as a matter of convenience, grouped the total number of deaths resulting from the plague. This convenient reporting is common enough today; no one is accused of error when it is claimed that 24,000 people died by an earthquake, if in fact 1,000 of them died as a result of starvation or cholera after the earthquake. Similarly, it is not incorrect to say that 450,000 men died fighting in the American Civil War, even though two thirds of these died from disease.

In Galatians 3:17 Paul implies that the time from God's promise to Abraham in Genesis 12:7 to the giving of the law at Sinai was 430 years. According to Exodus 12:40–41, 430 years was the exact time that the Israelites lived in Egypt. Paul, brought up as a strict Jew who knew his Old Testament thoroughly (Philippians 3:5), was hardly likely to make such an elementary mistake. A careful reading of Galatians 3:17 will show that Paul writes, 'the law, introduced 430 years later…' The question is, 'Later than what?' Paul did not write, 'later than the first giving of the promise to Abraham'. If in fact Paul means to imply 430 years after the patriarchal period—of Abraham, Isaac and Jacob—during which time the promise was often repeated, this would bring us to the beginning of Israel's exile in Egypt and would agree with Exodus 12:40–41.

In passing we should notice that Genesis 15:13 and Stephen in Acts 7:6 both refer to the period as one of 400 years. But this is merely rounding down the more precise figure in Exodus 12 and Galatians 3. We speak of the *King James Version* of the Bible being 'four hundred years old', whereas it is a few years over that.

STEPHEN'S OLD TESTAMENT HISTORY

In the previous chapter it was noted that Stephen referred to a tomb in Shechem which Abraham had purchased from the sons of Hamor (Acts 7:16). In this tomb Jacob and his sons were buried. But the only field that the Old Testament records Abraham buying was the field belonging to Ephron in Machpelah (Genesis 23:17). However, we may ask on what grounds we are to assume these two purchases were the same? Abraham purchased a field and cave in Machpelah in which he buried Sarah (Genesis 23), and in which he was himself buried (Genesis 25:9). He also purchased a tomb in Shechem (Acts 7). Jacob later purchased the entire field in which this was situated (Genesis 33:19; Joshua 24:32); in this cave in Shechem Jacob and his sons were buried.

In Acts 7:14 Stephen claimed that the number of Israelites that originally came into Egypt was 'seventy-five persons'. Genesis 46:27, Exodus 1:5 and Deuteronomy 10:22 all state that this figure was seventy. This is not a difficult problem to resolve because the Greek translation of the Old Testament (the *Septuagint*) gives the number in Genesis 46:27 and Exodus 1:5 as seventy-five persons, and Stephen was obviously following the Septuagint.

But does this mean that the Hebrew Old Testament was wrong? No, because in Genesis 46:20 a list of five grandsons of Joseph are added in the Greek *Septuagint*; these five are simply ignored in the Hebrew. In claiming that just seventy, or seventy-five, persons came into Egypt, both the Hebrew and Greek are referring to those whom they considered important heads of households. In fact many servants and other great-grandchildren must have come with them. The Hebrew Old Testament therefore lists only the sons and grandsons of Jacob and the number is seventy persons; the Greek Old Testament adds five great-grandsons. Both are correct.

MATTHEW'S OLD TESTAMENT HISTORY

In Matthew 27:9 an Old Testament quotation which appears to come from Zechariah is attributed to Jeremiah. But the passage in Zechariah 11:12–13 is considerably different from that in Matthew and since Matthew nowhere claims to be quoting from Zechariah, he may not be. Probably the best explanation is to notice that in the *Babylonian Talmud* (a book of Jewish laws and teaching just before and after the birth of Christ), Jeremiah is placed at the head of all the prophets (compare Matthew 16:14). Therefore, Matthew may have used Jeremiah as the general heading, just as we might say, 'Samuel tells us,' using the title of the book, when we actually refer to the words of Saul or David recorded within the book of Samuel.

Gospel differences

Some critics endeavour to find errors everywhere in the Gospels. That is precisely what Sir William Ramsay expected until the force of truth convinced him otherwise (chapter 2). In the light of the vast amount of material from the three-year ministry of Jesus that could have been included (John 20:31), it is remarkable how much is repeated in more than one of the Gospels. One contemporary writer pointedly concludes,

'The unity of the Synoptists' [the first three Gospels] witness to Jesus' life is much more impressive than its diversity. The fact that each evangelist remained highly selective in which details he chose to include in no way impugns the historical accuracy of the information which he did incorporate.' [118]

If the Gospel writers were aware of each other and made use of some common source or sources (as most critics assume), it is significant that they did not attempt to 'tidy up' the apparent discrepancies that they must have been aware of, or that the early church did not do this for them. Perhaps neither they nor the church saw these details as anything more than *apparent* discrepancies that could be readily understood.

---

118 Craig L Blomberg, *The Historical Reliability of the Gospels* (Apollos Publishing 2007), p. 131.

THE SERMON ON THE MOUNT

The differences between the sermon recorded in Matthew 5 –7 and that in Luke 6 present the critic with a reason for suggesting that we have two contradictory accounts of the same event. This is a superficial conclusion. The possibility that the two occasions are entirely different is unlikely. A more straightforward solution is that Matthew's phrase translated 'on a mountainside' (Matthew 5:1) can be properly translated 'into the hill country', and Luke's 'on a level place' (Luke: 6:17) refers to 'a plateau in mountainous regions.'[119] These are complementary phrases implying that we have the same event.

The occasional difference in wording in the teaching of Jesus (there are no contradictions) would be understood, as noted in the previous chapter, if he was teaching for some time and repeating himself as the crowd changed throughout the day. This possibility is too frequently overlooked when discussing the differences between the Gospels' report of Jesus' teaching. As has been noted before, we have only a small proportion of the full teaching content of Jesus' ministry and as crowds came and went there is no reason why, on the same occasion, he should not have repeated parables and teaching with slight variations.

THE CENTURION'S SERVANT

Matthew 8:5 informs us that as Jesus entered Capernaum, 'a centurion came to him asking for help' Luke 7:3 records that he sent 'some elders of the Jews to him'. The words 'came to him' in Matthew, which may be literally translated 'approached him', could simply express the sending of messengers; just as we would speak of a nation's leader making an 'approach' to another head of state without necessarily going in person. Compare Matthew 11:2–3 where John sent two of his disciples to Jesus and the words literally read: 'And [he] said to him…' (*English Standard Version*). The verb is singular, meaning that the Baptist is speaking through his messengers.

---

119 D A Carson, *Exegetical Fallacies*, 2nd ed. (Baker Books. Grand Rapids. MI, 1999). p. 43.

THE TEMPTATIONS OF JESUS

Matthew and Luke reverse the order of the last two temptations, but this would only be a contradiction if both claimed to present the correct order. Each closes with the temptation suited to his theme—Matthew is presenting Jesus as King, while Luke presents him as Man. Probably Matthew has the original order since he introduces his second temptation with 'then', while Luke connects the second and third merely with the word 'and'. There is no reason to assume that these three specific temptations all happened closely after each other; days may have intervened.

BLIND BARTIMAEUS

Matthew 20:30 mentions two blind men at Jericho, while Mark and Luke refer only to one (Mark 10:46; Luke 18:35). Luke also states the episode took place as Jesus 'approached' Jericho while Matthew and Mark claim he was 'leaving' Jericho.

Mark and Luke do not deny there were two men; they concern themselves only with one, Bartimaeus, perhaps because they focus on the one who was, or became, more well-known; this is implied by Mark's reference to the father of Bartimaeus (Mark 10:46). It is common for news commentators today to focus on the more notorious of those involved in an incident. Similarly, in another narrative Matthew refers to two demoniacs while Mark and Luke mention only one (Matthew 8:28 and Mark 5:2).

More significantly, did Christ heal at Jericho as they entered (Luke) or left (Matthew and Mark)?

Today, and in the time of Jesus, there is both the new Jericho and the ruins of the old Jericho—of Joshua fame—just outside the city. One explanation is that Jesus was in between the two when Bartimaeus was healed—thus he was leaving one and entering the other. This is the most simple and a possible explanation. Although some question whether a writer would refer to the old ruins when he knows his readers will be thinking of the city recently built by Herod.

Perhaps the whole episode should be reconstructed like this: The blind men were sitting in the entrance of the city and began calling to Jesus as he passed by. Jesus took no notice and the crowd ordered them to be silent. His refusal to stop and listen at once was not unusual in Jesus' ministry when he wanted to draw out a stronger appeal to himself; it is similar to the account of the Canaanite woman in Matthew 15:21–28. Jesus entered the city, met Zacchaeus and stayed at his home overnight. Later, the blind men crossed the city to renew their appeal as Jesus left in the morning. It was on this occasion that Jesus stopped and healed them.

This reconstruction assumes that the Gospel writers decided not to break up the story before and after Jesus' night in Jericho but to complete it as one event. Matthew and Mark recorded it on the departure because that is when the appeal was answered, and Luke dealt with it on the entry, because that is when the appeal began. If we take Luke 19:1, 'Jesus entered Jericho and was passing through', as a reference to the story of Bartimaeus and not the story of Zacchaeus, then we have Luke's way of telling us that the events he has just related actually took place as Christ came into and came out of the city—a perfect harmony with Matthew and Mark.

We do not have to prove that this is a correct reconstruction, only that it is reasonable and therefore quite possible. There is only a contradiction if we knew everything that could be known about the episode and still we could not harmonize the differences. If we are told of a friend who was killed in a terrible accident on the road, and subsequently discover that he died in hospital of his injuries a day later, we would not suggest that our first informant was either misinformed or misleading, he had simply not given us the full account. See the section on Harmonizing in the previous chapter.

THE FIG TREE WITHERED AND THE TEMPLE CLEANSED

Mark presents the chronological order of events: on the day of his triumphant entry into Jerusalem, Jesus went into the temple and saw what was happening; as it was late he returned with his disciples to Bethany. 'The next day as they were leaving Bethany', Jesus blighted the fruitless fig tree, then drove out the money-changers from the temple (Mark 11:11–19). It was the following morning when the disciples commented on the withered fig tree (20–25).

Matthew conflates the episode so that he can keep it as one uninterrupted account. He does not say which morning the blighting of the fig tree occurred, nor does his account demand that the comment by the disciples on the tree was on the same occasion as the blighting (Matthew 21:18–22). It is perfectly natural for Matthew to record the most significant activity of the day—cleansing the temple (vv. 12–17)—and then slip in a less significant event that began early one morning and was completed the following morning (vv. 18–22).

There is no contradiction between the two accounts, and it is incidents like this that reveal the complete independence of the Gospel writers from each other.

THE PARABLE OF THE TENANT FARMERS

In Mark 12:9 and Luke 20:15–16 Jesus answered his own question at the conclusion of the parable of the vineyard farmers: 'What will the owner of the vineyard do to them? He will come and kill those tenants and give the vineyard to others.' Matthew 21:41 records that the priests and Pharisees responded to his question with their answer: 'He will bring those wretches to a wretched end.' Which account is correct? Did Christ answer his own question, or did the Pharisees answer it for him? It is quite reasonable to assume that Jesus, having drawn the answer from his hearers, repeated their answer for emphasis—a not uncommon teaching method.

THE PARABLE OF THE SOWER

Matthew, Mark and Luke each use a different Greek word to refer to those who respond to the seed sown in the hearts of men. In the Gospels recorded in Greek, Matthew uses 'understand' (Matthew 13:23), Mark has 'accept' (Mark 4:20) and Luke adds 'retain' or 'hold fast' (Luke 8:15). If Jesus was preaching in Aramaic, we may assume that these three expressions (which are, incidentally, a natural progression) express all that our Lord originally had in mind. Additionally, as noted earlier, it is more than likely Jesus repeated this parable several times during his ministry, even on the same day and occasion, and each time he chose a different emphasis.

PETER'S DENIAL

The accounts of Matthew and Mark for Peter's denial of Christ correspond exactly, provided that we do not assume that 'the servant girl' in Mark 14:69 is the same as the one in verse 66, since Matthew refers to her as 'another girl' (Matthew 26:71). We may harmonize Luke's account (Luke 22:54–62) in the following way: The second maid identified Peter to the bystanders (Matthew 26:73 and Mark 14:69) and it was one of the men who confronted Peter (Luke 22:58). After a while, Luke says about an hour, the crowd challenged him again and all three Gospels agree in detail here. There is nothing in John's account (18:17,18,25–27) that conflicts with the above. John merely adds details that came to him from his better acquaintance with the people involved. There is certainly no need to resort to the suggestion that Peter denied his Lord on six occasions!

THE INSCRIPTION ON THE CROSS

The form of the inscription varies in each of the four Gospels. Matthew 27:37 records the written charge against him: 'This is Jesus, the King of the Jews.' Mark 15:26 has simply: 'The King of the Jews', and Luke 23:38 is similar, with the addition of one word (in the Greek): '*This is* the King of the Jews.' Clearly Mark went to the heart of the charge and ignored the rest; the others merely fill in. There is no conflict here. John 19:19, however, adds a much fuller record of the charge: 'Jesus of Nazareth, the King of the Jews.' The inscription was in three languages (according to John 19:20—Aramaic, Latin and Greek) therefore we must not only allow for some variation in translation, but it is more than likely that Pilate himself, or his secretary, was not consistent in using exactly the same inscription in all three languages. If John is reading from the Aramaic inscription, then the addition of the words 'of Nazareth' would have been a deliberate insult to the Jews by suggesting that their Jewish king came from that maligned city up north.

THE CRUCIFIXION ACCOUNTS

All four Gospels record in some detail the arrest, imprisonment, trials and crucifixion of Jesus. John alone uses the Gentile-Roman (Julian) timing as his reference which meant that his day began at midnight and 'about the sixth hour' (John 19:14), when Jesus was handed over to the Jews by Pilate, would be six in the morning. This is what we might expect since at the time of writing his Gospel he had been resident in Ephesus for many years and was writing particularly with Gentiles in mind. On the other hand, the Jewish day began at sunrise, about six in the morning. Therefore Mark's 'third hour when they crucified him' (Mark 15:25) would be nine in the morning and the 'sixth hour until the ninth hour' of Matthew 27:45; Mark 15:33; Luke 23:44 when darkness came over the land would be midday until three in the afternoon.

Professor Colin Humphreys undertook a thorough research into the last three days of Jesus' life and pieced together the events; he showed the remarkable convergence of all the details from the four Gospels.[120] His conclusion is that Jesus was arrested on Wednesday evening (not Thursday as traditionally thought) tried on Thursday and crucified on Friday 14 Nisan (our April 3) in the year AD 33.

THE THIEVES ON THE CROSS

Matthew and Mark inform us that the two robbers crucified with our Lord ridiculed him (Matthew 27:44; Mark 15:32) but Luke elaborates this to show that one had second thoughts and repented (Luke 23:39–43). Whether Matthew and Mark knew of this change is not significant; it clearly did not suit their purpose to record it. The value of these complementary accounts is that we know the repentant thief began by reviling Christ.

THE DEATH OF JUDAS

In an attempt to prove a contradiction in the Gospels, the difference between Matthew's account and Luke's is often referred to. Matthew 27:5 reports the end of the betrayer with the simple statement that 'He went away and hanged himself.' It is Luke who, in Acts 1:18–19, adds to Matthew's account and states that Judas 'bought a field' with his

---

120 Colin J Humphreys, *The Mystery of the Last Supper* (Cambridge University Press 2011). For a summary of his significant conclusions see Anderson and Edwards, *Evidence for the Bible* (Day One Publications, Leominster 2014), pp. 205–207.

ill-acquired money. He did, although it was never his intention. What happened was that the priests made the purchase for him, as Matthew 27:6–10 informs us. They bought the field in which he had committed suicide—and with his money. The events end on an even more gruesome note. When Judas hanged himself (Matthew 27:5) his body fell to the ground and broke open (Acts 1:18). When all parts of the story are pieced together, there is no contradiction. Each add a little more information.

THE RESURRECTION ACCOUNTS

The variation in the four resurrection narratives recorded in the Gospels has led many to conclude that we are faced with irreconcilable contradictions. Certainly a neat harmony may not be possible, but that there are no contradictions has been demonstrated by many commentators. Apparently neither the apostles, nor the early church, found any problem in recognising that we have various aspects of those fast-moving events from Friday to Sunday. Many have offered a coherent account and we must remember that in all biblical narratives there are always many more details that are not recorded.[121]

See in this series Book 1 chapters 3 to 5 for more on the authentic accuracy of the New Testament.

CONCLUSION

In this chapter an attempt has been made to discuss a sample of the issues that are raised against the accuracy of the biblical record. All the supposed errors and contradictions form only a very small part of the Bible. Whole chapters of historical recording contain nothing that even the most severe critic would dismiss. Not all responses may satisfy, but it is important to remember that the issue is not: 'Is the answer proved by every standard to

---

121 See *Evidence for the Bible*, pp. 208–210 for a composite of the Resurrection accounts. There have been many reconstructions of the Resurrection accounts, including: Frank Morison, *Who Moved the Stone?* (1930); Norman Anderson, *The Evidence for the Resurrection* (1950); John Wenham, *Easter Enigma—Do the Resurrection stories contradict one another?* (1984); N T Wright, *The Resurrection of the Son of God* (2003); Gary Habermas and Michael Licona, *The Case for the Resurrection of Jesus* (2004); Tom Bell, *The Miracle of the Third Day* (2016).

be right, without a shadow of a doubt?' but simply, 'Is it reasonable?' If it is reasonable then it may be right.

In Book 1 chapter 3 of this series, the principles set out in the nineteenth century by Simon Greenleaf, one of the founders of the Harvard Law School in America were discussed. It is worth repeating them in brief here:

- Documents, ancient or modern, have the right to be taken as a true and correct record unless and until proven otherwise: 'In trials of fact, by oral testimony, the proper inquiry is not whether it is possible that the testimony may be false, but whether there is sufficient probability that it is true.'

- The documents are most likely to be accepted as authentic if they are found to have come from the place and written by the people who would be most likely responsible for them.

- The character of the author of a document is to be considered trustworthy and credible unless or until it is proven otherwise.

- The number of independent witnesses confirms the greater likelihood of the accuracy of their report. And the agreement of their evidence significantly enhances the truth of their record.

- The reliability of a report is confirmed by the degree to which details match known events and circumstances.

The biblical documents, and in particular the New Testament, meet all these requirements.

At the close of his *Scientific Investigation into the Old Testament*, Robert Dick Wilson, the brilliant early twentieth century scholar referred to in chapter two, ended like this:

'We therefore send this volume forth with the prayer that it may strengthen the faith of those who still believe in God and in Jesus Christ His Son. We need not and do not fear the truth about the Bible. We welcome all sincere and honest study of its origin, purpose and meaning. But is it too much to ask and hope that more of those who have been appointed by the church to teach its history and its doctrines should devote their time and energies to the defence of its great and fundamental, unique and outstanding, facts and implications, rather than to the picking of flaws in the garments of the prophets and to the punching of holes in the robe of Christ's perfection? It may not be ours to remove all the difficulties, to harmonise all the apparent inconsistencies, to explain all the mysteries, and to solve all the problems of the Old Testament; but we can show at least, that we believe that Christ and the Apostles are more likely to be right than we, that the age-long judgement of the Church with respect to the Bible may after all be right, and that our business is to defend with all lawful means the citadel of faith rather than to join the hosts of the infidel in assaults upon its walls.'[122]

---

122 Robert Dick Wilson, *A Scientific Investigation of the Old Testament* (Marshall Brothers Ltd, London and Edinburgh, 1926), p. 214.

Index to significant subjects

These references will take the reader only to the book and chapter (eg 1/3, 4/5) in this series where the more significant references to the subject occur.

Index to significant subjects

Index to significant subjects

Index to main Scripture references

These references will take the reader only to the book and chapter (eg 1/3, 4/5) in this series where the more significant Scripture references occur.

EVIDENCE
for the BIBLE

Clive Anderson and
Brian Edwards

LARGE FORMAT HARDBACK
FULL COLOUR THROUGHOUT
225mm × 275mm
260pp | ISBN 978-1-84625-416-1
REF EFB4161 | £25.00

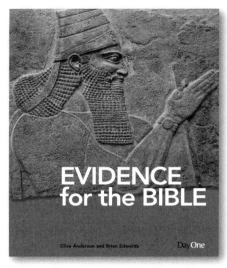

Evidence will surprise and inform you as you turn over the soil of history with the pages of your Bible. The witness of the trowel authenticates and illuminates the people and events, lifting them from the pages of the Book and setting them in the context of time and place. Join us on an exciting journey with this evidence from the past.

Evidence for the Bible can be found in many places, from the Ancient Near East to museums and private collections. Whilst artefacts can never prove the authority of the Bible, they can and do show that the events described in the Bible occurred in time and history.

This book provides a selection of the many items that demonstrate the reliability of the Bible as a historical document.

'Clive Anderson and Brian Edwards have captured the essence of generations of middle-eastern archaeology, historical context and biblical landscape in a quite remarkable way. Their book is accessible, informative and enjoyable. The pictures beautifully complement the text. The Bible comes alive. I warmly and wholeheartedly commend it to everyone who wishes to be a little wiser and better informed about the Book which has formed our culture and is the source of the Christian Faith.'

THE VERY REVD JAMES ATWELL,
Dean of Winchester.

'This is a marvellous introduction to the finds of archaeology that illumine our understanding of the Bible. It helps the reader to see that the biblical events and writings took place within history. When the reader studies the Bible, this book will serve as a wonderful tool to help get at its depth and richness. I highly recommend it.'

DR JOHN D CURRID
Carl McMurray Professor of Old Testament at the Reformed Theological Seminary, Charlotte, USA.

Additional commendations

'This superb series provides a set of quality tools, enabling every thoughtful Christian to know how to answer the Bible's critics and grow in their own confidence and appreciation of God's living and enduring Word. Packed with valuable factual information, detailed documentation, wide-ranging references and penetrating reasoning, not a sceptical stone is left unturned and not a critical argument goes unanswered.

Here is a comprehensive and greatly needed resource, which deserves to be required reading for every believer as we seek to live by God's inerrant revelation and present its message with authenticity to an unbelieving world. I could not commend the series more warmly.'

DAVID JACKMAN, *author, former President of the Proclamation Trust and founder of the Cornhill Training Course*

'A superb collection, readable and reliable, with lots of footnotes to check out the material presented. A terrific resource for both believers and those seeking faith. Students at Moorlands will love this series. Highly recommended!'

DR STEVE BRADY, *Principal, Moorlands College, Christchurch*

'*All you need to know about the Bible* blends apologetics, history and biblical studies to produce this important and hugely enjoyable series. It provides the reader with a mental landscape within which a confident and intelligent love for the Bible can be nurtured. It is a tour de force and a marvellous gift to the church in our secular age. I could not commend it more warmly or enthusiastically.'

RICHARD CUNNINGHAM, *Director, Universities and Colleges Christian Unions*

'Accessible throughout, these comprehensive introductory accounts of Scripture will be of immense value to everyone who reads them. They go far beyond a simple introduction and probe deeply into the nature of the Bible as the faultless Word of God, considering and answering a full range of criticisms. Moreover, Brian writes in a manner that will benefit the newest Christian. I hope his work receives the widest possible readership.'

DR ROBERT LETHAM, *Professor of Systematic and Historical Theology, Union School of Theology, Wales*

Additional commendations

'This series of attractive, accessible introductions offers a feast of wisdom and insight into the origins and accuracy of the Bible. When navigating the complex issues surrounding ancient texts and modern translations, here is an excellent place to begin—a helpful guide to the basics of history, archaeology and manuscript evidence. Most importantly, the series encourages us to delight afresh in the truthfulness, sufficiency and authority of God's Word. These volumes will be of assistance to every Bible student.'
DR ANDREW ATHERSTONE, *Latimer Research Fellow, Wycliffe Hall, Oxford*

'The overwhelming strength of Brian's comprehensive series is that it provides ordinary Christians with confidence in the authority of the Bible. Brian has the skill to make this subject accessible without simplification or omission. What a great resource for Christians, equipping us to be on the front foot when it comes to defending the Bible against its many detractors!'
ADRIAN REYNOLDS,
author, local church pastor and Training Director of the Fellowship of Independent Evangelical Churches

'Each one of these books is a valuable guide to the teaching and historical reliability of the Bible. Together, the set builds a compelling case for the authority of Scripture as the very words of God with life-changing power. A wealth of material in readable style, it is a rich resource, giving fresh confidence in the reliability and authority of the Scriptures.'
BILL JAMES,
Principal, The London Seminary

'Like a jeweller turning a diamond so that every facet flashes with light, Brian holds up God's Word so that its perfections shine. Although my views differ from his on Bible translations, these books serve well to answer helpfully numerous objections, confirm faith, and wisely guide in profitable reading of the Word.'
DR JOEL R. BEEKE,
President, Puritan Reformed Theological Seminary, Grand Rapids, Michigan